New Timber Architecture in Scotland

Peter Wilson

A registered architect for 25 years, Peter Wilson is Director of Business Development at Napier University's Centre for Timber Engineering. Over the past decade he has been responsible for the promotion of architectural competitions, lectures, seminars, conferences, exhibitions and demonstration projects that highlight innovation and design excellence in the use of timber. He writes regularly for *Building Design, Prospect* and *Timber Building magazine* and edited *'Designing with Timber', 'Timber Cladding in Scotland'* and *'Making the Grade - a guide to appearance grading UK grown hardwoods'* for arcamedia, a specialist publisher of technical material for construction industry professionals.

Published in 2007 by
arcamedia

8 Campbell's Close
Edinburgh EH8 8JJ
Scotland.
T +44 (0)131 556 7963
F +44 (0)871 263 6714
E enquiries@arcamedia.eu
W www.arcamedia.eu

A catalogue record for this book is available from the British Library.

ISBN 978-1-904320-05-0

Designed by Alan Mairs.
Printed by Howies.
Cover photograph of Robin House, Balloch by Andrew Lee.

New Timber Architecture in Scotland

This publication began life as an idea for a small catalogue of new timber buildings. That it expanded into a book containing projects built throughout the length and breadth of Scotland might be attributed to author enthusiasm, but more accurately to the sheer number of examples discovered in the course of research. Inevitably, as more and more good projects emerged, the time taken to assemble material on them became extended, and it is to the credit of Forestry Commission Scotland, who initiated the project, that the final result is as comprehensive as it is. James McDougall, the Commission's Promotion & Development Officer in its Perth & Argyll Conservancy has been a particular strength in bringing the publication to fruition, and indeed it would not have emerged at all without his energy, understanding and ability over the long period of its gestation to keep the project's many interested parties focused on the final outcome. Thanks too need to be extended to Forestry Commission Scotland's Derek Nelson, John Dougan and Keith Wishart, all of whom contributed in no small part from their respective areas of responsibility to the project. Roger Coppock, the Commission's Policy Advisor, Business Development also deserves acknowledgement and thanks for nurturing the project through its final stages.

Cedric Wilkins at Scottish Enterprise's Forest Industries Cluster also contributed to the development of the publication, whilst Ivor Davies, at the Centre or Timber Engineering at Napier University, patiently responded to my endless technical queries, whether in the areas of wood science or construction. For publisher arcamedia, Alan Mairs worked tirelessly to deliver a design that draws together the huge amount of text and illustrations into a coherent and visually striking whole.

I have also been fortunate to enjoy the trust of the agencies, organizations and individuals referred to above to deliver this summary of new timber architecture in Scotland. I would emphasise, therefore, that all of the statements, opinions and interpretations expressed in the text are mine alone and should not be seen as having been approved or endorsed by any of these parties. The same is true of any factual and/or technical accuracy and if errors have found their way into the text, I am the responsible party and can only apologise for them in advance.

In the end, however, this publication would not have been possible without the generous contribution of time and material from two particular groups of people – the architectural practices whose projects are represented in these pages, and the photographers whose sterling work shows these buildings at their best. The members of these groups are individually listed in the rear of the publication, but it is their collective commitment and passion to produce work of outstanding quality that has made the writing, design and production of 'New Timber Architecture in Scotland' such an inspiring experience.

Peter Wilson,
November 2007

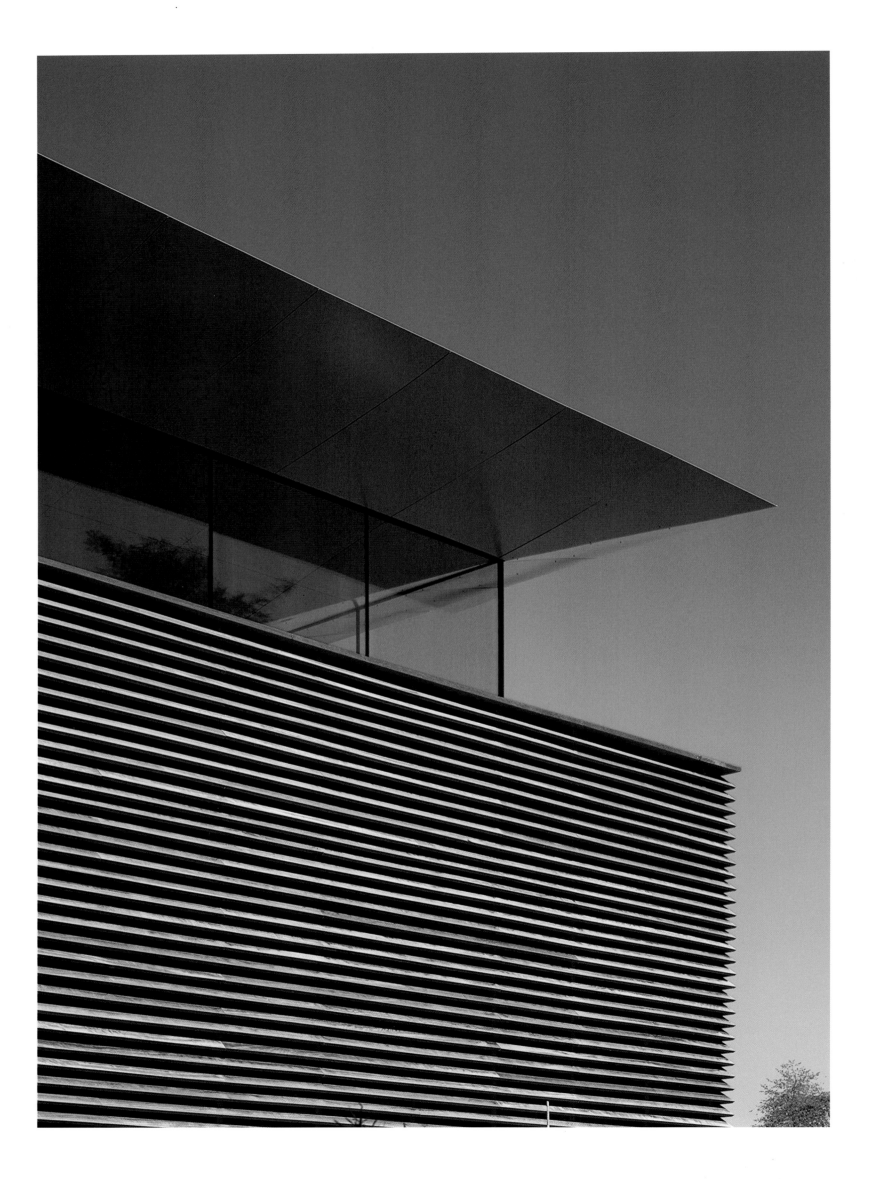

Contents

◄ Visitor Centre,
   Mount Stuart, Isle of Bute.

Foreword

Much has happened in the architecture and built environment of Scotland in the six years or so since Forestry Commission Scotland initiated the publication of *'Designing with Timber'*. At that time both the Commission and Scottish Enterprise were concerned to encourage more specification of timber – and in particular, home-grown wood – by Scottish architects and others within the domestic construction industry. The main themes within that publication – sustainability, certification and specification, design innovation, and the availability of construction-quality timber from Scotland's forests – are as relevant now as they were then. The big change since that time, however, is that we can now see a tremendous number of new buildings around Scotland that make exemplary use of timber. This can only be a good thing: we have the largest forest resource in the UK and stimulating more use of home-grown timber in new construction is not only environmentally sensible, it makes a significant contribution to the well-being of our rural economy.

Through a number of initiatives, strategies and publications, Forestry Commission Scotland, Scottish Enterprise and the relevant departments and agencies of the Scottish Government have been pro-active in emphasising these points and it is very evident that the architectural and construction community here no longer needs to be convinced of the efficacy of using timber: quite simply, they are doing it. The challenge now is to demonstrate to other sections of our community the benefits that can be realised from making more use of this renewable natural resource. This new publication catalogues many of the best projects that have been constructed throughout Scotland during the past few years, not only to indicate the diversity of building types on which timber has been used, but more importantly to make clear that wood is not at all an unusual or inappropriate material to use in our variable climate.

I am sure many people will be pleasantly surprised by the range and sheer number of good buildings illustrated in *'New Timber Architecture in Scotland'*. I hope like me, they will also feel proud that ever greater numbers of projects as good as these are emerging in Scotland. Exemplary timber architecture is nowadays not only to be found in those other countries of Europe that have extensive forest resources: it is here, it is sustainable and it is making a major contribution to the quality of the built landscape of Scotland.

Dr Bob McIntosh
Director, Forestry Commission Scotland.

Introduction

'New Timber Architecture in Scotland' would have been inconceivable ten years ago and it is a measure of the extent to which things have changed in only a decade that such a comprehensive summary of recent timber projects has been possible. 90 exemplar buildings and structures have been selected to show that timber is not an unusual material to use in contemporary building design, whether rural or urban. The publication might also be regarded as a review of the role of timber in the architectural culture of modern Scotland and a signpost to where this may go in the future. The projects encompass almost every building type – public, residential, commercial, education, health, sport, leisure, culture & tourism. Many of the architectural practices whose work is included here have very obviously made a virtue of designing with timber and in doing so have gained considerable experience in its use. Others have made tentative steps towards greater specification of timber in their work and cladding with wood has become, for many designers and builders, the low threshold entry point to learning about the one construction material that can genuinely be described as renewable.

Encouragingly, research for this publication uncovered a considerable number of projects currently either in the early stages of design or awaiting planning approval or in construction and due for completion at some stage within the next 18 months. Many of these might be described as being part of a 'Phase II' of contemporary timber building in Scotland: technically more assured and more inventive in the many ways in which timber has been considered during the design process. No longer regarded as a cheap-looking material with a short life-span, in this new age of environmental concern and desire for more sustainable forms of construction, timber has risen to become an important material of choice for even those buildings that command the appellation 'high-tech'.

◁ The Bridge Arts Centre,
   Easterhouse, Glasgow.

▷ Falkirk Wheel Visitor Centre.

A quick glance through these pages demonstrates that there is no single style nor even any obviously individual approach that in the past might have been described as distinctively 'Scottish'. The reason for this is simple: timber having long been out of use as a primary construction material, Scotland's architects, engineers, builders – and even building owners – have had to learn from first principles about its many properties and to achieve technical proficiency have sensibly elected to eschew stylistic considerations. In this respect, time-honoured techniques as well as lessons from abroad are much in evidence, but modern regulations and building processes have also demanded a degree of innovation based on new scientific research and a radical rethink of the ways in which we grow timber and the methods we use to extract wood from the forest to produce modern building materials.

In the course of this, old prejudices and sometimes even profound ignorance have had to be overcome. The general public, politicians, planning and building control officers, funding providers and even material suppliers have, until now, been in the slipstream of the educational journey that many architects, engineers, quantity surveyors and builders have already undertaken. The purpose of this publication is to transfer some of this knowledge, to provide confidence, and to excite and inspire others to demand or to make use of timber in new building projects. Old excuses for avoiding a material we have in abundance ("we don't have the right climate", "we grow the wrong type of timber", etc.) no longer bear serious scrutiny.

What is required now is greater openness to designs utilising timber and a clear recognition that more training and practice in this area will help to ensure the country's built environment is improved in a genuinely sustainable way. We are now seeing considerable innovation in the areas of timber engineering and construction and, through this, the emergence of new building types that could only have been created here. The next phase of Scotland's timber architecture is likely to be even more distinctive, but far from being a post-devolution search for a national style these new architectural solutions are appearing in response to prevailing regional characteristics and the requirement for new building types. Creating many more of them from the country's own forest resource is the next significant challenge.

Stirling Cricket Club, Stirling.

The Detached House in the North

Demographic and social change have stimulated debate about the kind of housing stock needed to meet 21st century demands. At one end of the spectrum there are more young, single people and one-parent families keen to move into affordable modern homes, whilst at the other end of the age scale, people are living longer and looking for dignified, secure places in which to stay. Extended families, second homes and the buy-to-let market have all contributed to revisions in our thinking about housing design. Other factors too have impacted upon our perceptions of architecture and its value to daily domestic life. Television makeover programmes have brought the idea of continuous renewal and design adventure into the way we shape our homes, whilst increased ecological awareness has concentrated attention on the waste we create as a society and the need for houses which are far more environmentally-friendly in their design and use of materials.

Given these circumstances, it is hardly surprising that demand has increased for alternatives to the expensive and all-too-often bland properties offered by volume developers; equally it is no accident that greater amounts of timber are appearing on the exterior of houses, rather than being used only for the building's internal (and unseen) structure. Good examples of individually designed, environmentally responsive houses can now be found throughout Scotland, with more being encouraged by both government and local planning authorities. The Scottish Executive's Planning Advice Note 72, 'Housing in the Countryside' makes clear the economic and practical advantages of timber frame construction and timber cladding, even including explicit encouragement for greater use of the latter. Changed days indeed from the bleak period prior to the end of the 20th century when insensitively designed kit-built homes were allowed to disfigure the rural landscape.

Nowhere is this change more evident than in the Highland and Grampian regions of Scotland, areas of spectacular natural beauty in which seemingly endless tracts of bleak, bare landscape are matched in other parts by vast expanses of woodland cover. In recent years a new generation of architect-designed timber homes has been built across this huge area – not only in or beside the forested zones, but also on the wilder coastal edges and islands. Houses built of timber in these locations are arguably far more climatically challenged than in any other part of the UK; the fact that so many of those built in recent years continue to perform well indicates a new-found optimism amongst architects that is based on sound technical practice and a better understanding of the properties of natural materials.

Seminal in this transformed perception of timber's qualities was the house designed by Gokay Deveci at Durness in Sutherland for Danish ceramicist Lotte Glob. Sitting on the shore of Loch Eriboll, the building's timber post and beam structure is designed to withstand winds of up to 120kmph that come sweeping across the water in winter. The external wall cladding is formed from rough sawn shiplap boarding of untreated Scottish oak and makes a striking contrast to the highly controlled precision of the house's laminated timber roof structure. Using this kind of highly engineered and prefabricated kit of timber

Lotte Glob House,
Loch Eriboll, Durness, Sutherland.

'Ceol Mara', Loch Broom, Wester Ross

⌄ Lotte Glob House,
   Loch Eriboll, Durness, Sutherland.

parts makes it possible for unskilled workers to assemble affordable structures and components in any location – an important factor for such a remote site. To some, the house's long plan and curved copper roof may appear jarringly non-traditional, but the vernacular architecture of Sutherland is made up of croft buildings and agricultural sheds that sit harmoniously into the landscape. The architect's approach here has been to combine his response to the latter with visual elements of this indigenous architecture. In his own words, "the landscape is both a view, something you take in, and your immediate physical surroundings, something you are taken in by".

South of here, on the shores of Loch Broom near Ullapool, sits 'Ceol Mara', another timber-framed and clad dwelling or, more accurately, two pavilions linked together to form one house. Designed by Bernard Planterose of Northwoods Construction Ltd, the building's complex groundworks wrap around the contours of the site with the front of each pavilion raised on stilts above the sloping ground. The two distinct elements – an open plan living, kitchen and dining area and the three storey bedroom block – are respectively oriented to harness the dual views of mountains and loch, and are distinguished externally by their different uses of European larch cladding. The white-stained timber on the bedroom block is fixed horizontally whilst the grey stained external skin of the living area combines vertical board-on-board cladding with off-saw planks that have been roughly dressed and chamfered.

A little further to the southwest, a number of refined, modern timber homes have appeared on Skye in recent years. Designed to complement the island's vernacular traditions, these new houses have challenged the hegemony of the kit-builders who, over many years, have so catastrophically impacted on the island's landscape with their anarchic scatter of misinterpreted indigenous building forms and features. One architectural practice – Dualchas – has been in the forefront of new house building on the island, producing a continuous string of one and two storey homes that are knitted sensitively into their sites and which introduce more appropriate contemporary technological responses to the environmental extremes that were the driver of the island's characteristic building style.

The results are simple, well-detailed and well-proportioned timber framed – and often timber clad – buildings, as can be seen in the practice's design for a new-build guesthouse at Harrapool, near Broadford. Given that this business type is a mainstay of the island's economy, there are remarkably few good modern examples to be found, but set back from the main road leading from the Skye Bridge, the building's deceptive simplicity distinguishes it immediately from its unremarkable neighbours. Planning restrictions meant this four bedroom house had to be kept low, and by cutting into the site the ground floor has been set at shore level. The approach to the front door gives notice, however, that this long, slate-roofed project is not a conventional two storey solution – a bridged walkway leads to the upper floor entrance, with the door set into a recessed timber-clad plane that emphasises the design's horizontality. The small first floor glazing units also sit within this grey-painted panel, with the rest of the wall a contrasting, more traditional white render. This elevation also reveals the house's internal planning via the very visible row of rooflights set above the entrance hall and stair. On the other side of the house, by contrast, the living spaces and bedrooms have large planes of glazing to take advantage of the light and the view out to sea.

This is not rocket science, but rather the work of architects who care deeply about the landscape and context in which they build and whose own homes are exemplars of their work. Mary Arnold Forster, a partner in Dualchas, has made her house at Tokavaig into an economical exercise in timber design, using larch from Fort Augustus for its external cladding and shutters and local oak for the interiors. Similarly, Alan Dickson of Rural Design, another Skye-based practice, has eschewed typical panel construction and opted instead for a structure that uses standard-sized Douglas fir sections for the columns, flitch and ridge beams. This framing method allowed the entire one and a half storey height of his Milovaig home to be expressed internally, whilst its larch-clad 'pop-outs' give external expression to the stair and kitchen areas. Deliberately simple, but undeniably modern, Dickson's house at 'Milovaig' wears its skin of white-painted Norway spruce with confidence and is a well-detailed model of good timber cladding practice.

Shed, Tokavaig, Isle of Skye.

Guest House, Harrapool, Isle of Skye.

Dickson House, Milovaig, Isle of Skye.

Red House, Ross-shire.

Back in Ross-shire, a little north of Inverness, a different interpretation of the local vernacular has produced a strong response to a relatively featureless site. The house, by architects Brennan & Wilson, is set back against the established tree cover and anchored along the north boundary wall. Over and above the client's requirement for four bedrooms, the building has been designed to accommodate a substantial art collection. The architectural language of traditional Scottish agricultural buildings has been adopted here to generate the necessary internal wall space and to produce a series of pitched gable-end roofs that step back to provide sheltered protection from the prevailing south-west wind. The large window openings in this south facade take advantage of solar gain and maximise the views, at the same time expressing the building's contemporary domestic credentials. And, to extend its durability and to provide a homogeneous appearance under weathering, the meticulously detailed cladding has been painted the same rustic red colour that is commonly used on large agricultural structures in the Scottish countryside.

Still in the area around Inverness, architect Neil Sutherland has for several years been constructing timber houses for individual clients, each a singular contrast to the hectares of anonymous homes being developed to service the accommodation needs of what is reputed to be the UK's fastest growing city. In this frenetic environment, experienced tradesmen with a real understanding of timber's physical properties are at a premium and, after many frustrating experiences, the architect set up his own sawmill and building company to provide the materials and craft skills needed to deliver his projects successfully. Each house has a strong ecological bent, the turf roofs of early projects superseded in more recent projects by profiled Eternit sheets redolent of the region's vernacular history. The design motivation for these houses is entirely consistent with current attitudes to energy usage and environmental responsibility, a good example being the modest dwelling at Balnafoich. Tucked discreetly into an area of dense woodland, its external walls are vertically clad with slow grown and practically knot free larch from a nearby estate, the house's modernity signalled by its curved green roof.

Across country, the planning constraints placed upon new buildings within the spectacular landscape of the Cairngorm National Park present unusual challenges for designers. 'Inchdryne', designed by Bernard Planterose and Locate Architects, was built to be an all-year holiday letting business part-funded by a grant from the Scottish Executive Environment and Rural Affairs Department under the Agricultural Business Diversification Scheme that is designed to support crofters and farmers and their immediate families. With a site backed on three sides by woodland, the client's brief to the design team was for a sustainable and ecologically sound house constructed entirely from Scottish grown timber. The result is an internally exposed main frame of Douglas fir, a secondary structure fabricated from spruce, and all of the external cladding produced from Highland-grown European larch. The cladding has been painted to contrast with the colour of the house's main frame. All of the timber is untreated, with only natural oil, paint or wax finishes used on the interior surfaces. And, with a reasonably open view to the south, two storey high glazing has been used on that side of the house as part of a passive solar heating strategy.

Nearby, close to Grantown-on-Spey, 'Wester Tombain' also displays a commitment to sustainable design and the use of locally sourced materials. The project initially encountered some opposition because its architecture was deemed 'too contemporary' for the National Park area, but the final result eloquently contradicts this perception and is an outstanding example of how to set a new building sensitively within its landscape. The site itself offers extraordinary panoramic views over the Cairngorm mountains, and MAKE Architects have taken advantage of these in the layout of the house. Living, dining, kitchen and bedroom accommodation as well as a garage are contained in a linear, south facing larch clad wing that sits on the footprint of a ruined stone steading. At right angles to this, the remainder of the former L-shaped building now contains the other four bedrooms required by the brief. The social area/circulation link that connects the two parts of the house is provided by a glazed internal sunspace that opens onto an external, south-facing timber deck. Externally, the vertically-lapped larch cladding will weather to match the monopitch zinc roof and complement the reclaimed granite and slate of the steading.

Also using the site of a previous building – this time a derelict, 100 year old timber-clad cottage – the Burnett House designed by architect Gokay Deveci on the Crathes Castle estate on Royal Deeside is an outstanding example of how to make a new dwelling as super-insulated and airtight as possible. And with 450mm of insulation in its roof and almost 300mm in the innovative double-stud timber-frame walls, triple glazing, Velux solar panels and a heat recovery system, this is a genuine zero energy/ zero carbon emissions house that has no need for a dedicated heating system. Yet this is not a house that wears its sustainable credentials on its sleeve – from the outside it seeks to empathise with local vernacular traditions, whilst taking the external use of timber to new levels of sophistication. The crisply articulated rainscreen cladding system uses 50mm square larch sections set 10mm apart to allow air to circulate freely. This open-joint effect also allows the cladding to pass in front of windows, allowing light to enter into the more private areas of the house.

Inchdryne Lodge, Nethy Bridge.

Onwin-Lawrence House,
Balnafoich, near Inverness.

Wester Tombain, Grantown-on-Spey.

Burnett House, near Banchory,
Royal Deeside.

The Detached House in Central and Southern Scotland

The domestic architecture of the Highland and Grampian regions is not separated in some stylistic or even philosophical sense from that found in the centre and south of Scotland; nor can it yet be said that there are discernible regional variations in the timber architecture found on either side of some invisible line drawn midway across the country. Certainly, the same determination to build excellent sustainable alternatives to the mainstream of speculative housing is evident in the examples from central and southern Scotland that are included here, but there are some important differences, not the least being the nature of the client base. For many, the opportunity to build a detached home for themselves and their families is only possible within commuting distance of the metropolitan areas that provides them with their employment, business and family contacts and friends. The requirement is perhaps more suburban in nature, but without any concomitant desire to live in an actual suburb. In part this desire to move away from town is down to the availability and cost of building land, but it is also a lifestyle choice, a desire for more space and family freedom.

Combining cosmopolitan sensibilities with environmental responsibility does not necessarily carry a financial premium, however, and indeed most of the examples included here are spectacularly good value on a cost per square metre basis. Nevertheless, the question of how to finance a project continues to be a real issue in many instances. For banks, building societies and mortgage providers more used to conventional house purchase options, building new and using timber is too often still regarded as high risk, and while the situation is gradually changing, the funding options available can still be frustratingly limited.

That said, some architects have made a virtue of cost-effective construction, even combining research into the use of materials with investigation into ways of building healthier houses. At Dalguise in Perthshire, Arc Architects set out to produce a single storey, three-bed home using external timber cladding on a timber frame backed by 200mm of insulating newspaper pulp and unfired earth bricks and with a thick clay plaster coat for the internal walls. This innovative, breathable wall construction not only achieves high levels of acoustic and thermal insulation, but also passively controls the relative humidity of the internal air to a level between 40 – 60% and impedes moisture condensation in the bathrooms to such an extent as to make the use of extract fans unnecessary. The result of this exercise in low-budget eco-building is a home that cost less than £650 per square metre to build, and a hard-to-beat model for genuinely affordable, healthy housing in the countryside.

Housing research takes many forms, and the development of replicable alternatives to the ubiquitous 'kit house' has become the architectural equivalent of the search for the Holy Grail. New models not only need to be competitively priced against the average equivalent new-build house, they also have to be capable of adaptation to a wide range of site conditions. Further economies as well as improvements can be tweaked out in each new manifestation of a prototype design, as evidenced by architect Mark

Laggan House, Blanefield.

Walker's own home at Glenalmond in Perthshire, and the subsequent version built in 2005 at Langwood Barn near Peebles. With echoes of the agricultural and light industrial barns found throughout Scotland's rural environment, these spacious properties occupy around half an acre of land each and make maximum use of high quality standard components to provide open plan living for around £600 per square metre at the time of building. Despite this low cost, there are subtle refinements in the details – the timber used externally, for example, is adjusted in size, orientation and finish according to its position on the house. The pitch of each roof determines the gauge at which the treated cedar shingles have been laid, whilst the house's living spaces are horizontally clad with smooth planed 125mm western red cedar boards that have been stained ebony black to give the feel of joinery rather than carpentry. The gable end timbers, by contrast, are rough sawn, untreated and fixed vertically, board-on-board. And, depending upon whether they are wet or dry, the roof shingles fluctuate in tone from dark to light, mediating between the colours of the different wall surfaces.

2 Kirk Park, Dalguise, Perthshire.

 Cedar House, Chapelhill, Logiealmond, Perthshire.

➢ Langwood Barn, near Peebles.

To some eyes, wooden shingles may seem an unusual cladding material for new houses but there is ample historical evidence of their use on rural and urban buildings in Scotland. Traditionally handcrafted, they had all but disappeared in this country in the face of factory manufactured products, but their continuing use across Europe and north America together with the availability of competitively-priced imported supplies of consistent quality has led to a reinvestigation of their benefits and design potential. Architects StudioKAP inventively employed them on a 'garden shed' as part of Glasgow's Year of Architecture in 1999, and subsequently to exemplary effect on a house extension in Bearsden. The practice's more recent Leijser House in Balfron (as seen on Channel 4's 'Grand Designs') takes the material deeper into modern design territory, using shingles on all four sides of a simple cubic form to distinguish the 4-bed, timber frame house from its unprepossessing neighbours. The timber frame itself comes from Sweden and has been tailored by the architects to achieve three things: a rich variety of internal spaces with an endlessly changing quality of natural light; exquisitely framed views of the surrounding landscape, with window openings punched out to permit seating in the reveals; and high insulatio levels to reduce to an absolute minimum the amount of energy used for heating.

Leijser House, Balfron.

At Seton Mains in East Lothian, a different approach to the non-standard use of timber frame technology has produced another crisply detailed house. Built by the architects, Paterson Associates, for their own family use, the form appears simple – this time a rectangular box. Again, one of the determining design factors has been the framing of views from a first floor living area, but such a straightforward analysis would be to understate the many subtleties of its architecture. The building's plan is extremely compact, placing all of the bedrooms on the ground floor in order that the living areas are able to take advantage of the view across the adjacent farmland to Aberlady Bay. The first floor space is awash with natural light and, with its open plan arrangement, appears much bigger than it actually is. In part, this perception is achieved by the use of additional windows in the roof, and in part by rethinking the proportions of the room to increase its height beyond that of conventional timber frame modules. The glazing units too are non-standard items, rising almost floor to ceiling and more elegantly proportioned than their commercial counterparts, a design decision that is also more than adequately justified by the external appearance of the building. In combination with vertical board-on-board untreated western red cedar cladding, the heightened windows provide the classical feeling of a *piano nobile* over the lower, more cellular ground floor plan.

➢ The Long House, Kilcreggan, Roseneath Peninsula, Argyll.

Paterson House, Seton Mains, Longniddry, East Lothian.

Whilst platform timber frame, in its many variations, now dominates domestic construction in Scotland, there are many examples of houses in which wood has been used in combination with other materials to good effect. The Long House at Kilcreggan in Argyll by Bl@st Architects is an unusual example of modern technology meeting traditional 'green' timber structural framing to produce a house with unique internal qualities. Another project given national exposure on 'Grand Designs', the house is sited on steeply sloping land with spectacular views down the Roseneath Peninsula, a location that required substantial concrete foundations upon which to raise the building's main frame. The resulting structure is a hybrid of steel and oak, the latter a traditional cruck frame with morticed joints and wooden pegs skilfully crafted by Carpenter Oak and Woodland. As such, the project could hardly be described as using standard components, since each timber element required to be selected for shape and curvature in the forest before felling. Marrying this historical technology to the precision of stainless steel has produced a remarkable and highly original house in which the upper floors convey all the light and spatial quality we associate with modern architecture whilst the structure recalls the best of this country's agricultural and religious buildings.

At Blanefield, in the shadow of the Campsie Fells and within commuting distance of Glasgow, jm architects' use of steel framing sits more firmly within the modernist tradition established in the 1920's by the famous German, Mies van der Rohe – off-site precision manufacturing and subsequent assembly of a kit of parts in which the I-beam structural elements are both articulated and exposed. With windows, balustrades and roof also of grey metal, the western red cedar wall panels, set within the grey-painted steel frame, are intended to provide a brief contrast in colour that will diminish in time as the timber responds to the local weather conditions. With its extended timber deck, the house itself appears to float above the gently sloping site, but as the cladding progressively mellows in tone from reddish-brown to grey, so too will the long, low house stand out less against its woodland backdrop.

And, at the end of this survey of new timber houses in Scotland that has drawn on examples from as far north as Lotte Glob's house and pottery workshop near Durness, the final project is the Holm at Orchardton in Dumfriesshire, coincidentally also a house for an internationally-acclaimed potter, Will Levi Marshall, who – as an 'official asset to Dumfries and Galloway' – was granted planning permission solely on the condition that he built a studio and that the house was his personal family home. The location however, is as different from the exposed coastal conditions of northern Sutherland as can be imagined: hidden in the Galloway Hills a few miles from the Solway Firth, the house and studio sit on a relatively flat paddock surrounded on all sides by trees. To maximise light, shelter and views, the single storey, four bedroom house is positioned in the north east corner of the 2.25 hectare site, with the living areas looking to the south west. The studio/pottery sits at right angles to the living area to create an enclosure to the parking area and entrance forecourt as well as screening to the private garden. The architects, Crallan & Winstanley, have employed a language of semi-industrial elements for the L-shaped house and adjacent pottery, an approach made most obvious in the metal glazing frames and expressed steel structure of the living area. The latter supports uncoated Douglas fir joists and plywood decking which, together with the timber of the floor and the built-in furniture, provide material continuity with the adjacent timber-framed and western red cedar-clad bedroom wing and pottery pavilion.

Laggan House, Blanefield.

The Holm, Orchardton, Dumfriesshire.

The Workplace

The modern workplace comes in many forms, but in recent years the sustainable specification and construction of new projects has climbed higher and higher on the agenda of clients, designers and end users. Rising energy costs have played their part in this, but so too has increased public awareness of the impact on the environment of the places in which they work. Changing attitudes have led to revisions and additions to construction legislation and these in turn have fostered new approaches in all areas of building design. In this more ecologically-conscious climate, emphasis – and value – is moving away from calculations of gross and net floor areas to ones of operational and economic performance and, most importantly, to quantification of the actual workspace quality experienced by a building's users.

In this respect, the architecture of business parks can all-too-often be uninspiring: low-cost speculative office space anonymous in appearance and unimaginative in the relationship to the landscape in which it is situated. The materials used have tended to be industrial in manufacture and appearance, providing uniformity rather than any distinctive qualities that would allow individual buildings to stand out. Aside from the vagaries of architectural fashion, this particular approach to specification can be ascribed in part to the fact that the end user is not the client and therefore unable to influence the design at an early development stage. In part it can also be attributed to the developer's need to maximise floor space, all-too-often unfortunately at the expense of the quality of the eventual working environment. The Gyle, at on Edinburgh's western edge, offers something of a catalogue of post-war business/industrial park development, ranging from older sites where masterplanning has been on a plot-by-plot basis, to the *tabula rasa* layout of Edinburgh Park by Richard Meier. Within the former context sits the Pentad development, a real attempt to raise the commercial appeal of a landscape dominated by mediocre

◁ Scottish Natural Heritage
    headquarters,
    Great Glen House, Inverness.

➤ Pentad, South Gyle, Edinburgh.

offices and faceless industrial sheds. Page\Park Architects' pinwheel layout of six proposed buildings for its client, the EDI Group, set out to create a new hub for the park and to provide the plan's road-edge buildings with distinctive character and presence. This is achieved by the use of a full-height colonnade along the front elevation of Block A to inflate its three-storey scale, an effect emphasised by the vertical western red cedar cladding on the main wall of the block itself. With the benefit of hindsight, this was a brave move since, even four years ago, the general image of an office building rarely conjured up the use of timber.

Times change, however, and since then a widening concern for the environment has stimulated serious reconsideration of the way in which office buildings are designed in order to find financially viable and sustainable construction solution. Rising fuel costs in particular have prompted demand for more energy efficient offices, an area in which HAA Design Ltd has been active for some years. The practice's recently completed Torus Building at the Scottish Enterprise Technology Park in East Kilbride is a two-storey speculative office pavilion designed to house a variety of individual companies. Environmental considerations lie at the heart of the building's conception, with a shared central atrium integral to a daylighting and natural ventilation strategy. The project secured a 'very good' BREEAM rating, the current UK standard measure of a building's sustainable design credentials. In this instance, materials with a low carbon impact are combined with high thermal insulation standards and energy-efficient construction,

Torus Building, Scottish Enterprise Technology Park, East Kilbride.

mechanical services and controls to produce top quality office accommodation. The horizontally-fixed western red cedar cladding on the building's exterior has been left uncoated to allow it to weather to grey and to minimize chemical treatments and attendant maintenance issues.

The use of timber in the construction of new office buildings is nowadays more than simply an external cladding option, however, and in their design for a two-storey, 2100 sq.m. business incubation centre on Livingston's Alba Campus, architects 3DReid have utilised products and systems normally found in the industrial and residential sectors to deliver an environmentally-conscious, cost efficient building that challenges accepted models without compromising BCO standards for offices. By using glulam for the main structural frame (a material that consumes only 10% of the energy used in the manufacture of a comparable steel solution) the architects have also been able to expose the warmth of the timber internally, whilst the use of TJI joist technology with plywood sheeting for the first floor (as commonly used in residential development) has provided an eco-friendly alternative to concrete planks or a poured concrete slab, again with significant energy savings in the manufacturing process. Scottish-grown European larch cladding has been fixed horizontally on the approach elevation to an inner leaf of prefabricated insulated timber panels. Factory manufactured solutions together with an almost total elimination of wet trades were used throughout the project to reduce excessive on-site waste and to improve the health and safety conditions for construction workers.

Torus Building, Scottish Enterprise Technology Park, East Kilbride.

Business Incubation Centre, Alba Campus, Livingston, West Lothian.

Innovative sustainable design in new office environments is not only found in the private sector, however, and in recent years several of Scotland's larger public agencies have been the enlightened clients for new headquarter premises for themselves. Indeed, the Scottish Public Pensions Agency (SPPA) was something of a pioneer when, as part of the Scottish Executive's relocation policy, it commissioned a purpose-built 3000 sq.m. single-storey office for its 170 staff on the banks of the River Tweed on the outskirts of Galashiels. The brief given to architects and engineers, RMJM Ltd, stipulated that the new building should meet very high standards of sustainability and that its form and materials should be appropriate to the rural setting. The result is a remarkable and efficient synthesis of energy and ecological considerations in an architectural and landscaping solution that is a model for out-of-town workplaces. The environmental strategy for the western red cedar clad building includes a green roofing system made with sedum matting that provides excellent thermal insulation and high rainwater retention. These features, coupled with a pond around the building, a self-draining car park and the use of indigenous plants in the landscape design, improve the biodiversity of the site and help minimise the impact of the facility on its immediate environment.

Scottish Natural Heritage was also required by the Scottish Executive to relocate its headquarters, in this instance moving its base of operations 120 miles north from Edinburgh to Inverness. When completed, the 6700 sq.m. Great Glen House by Keppie Design achieved a highest-ever BREEAM rating of 84% in recognition of its re-use of materials from an existing structure for aggregate and the use of A-rated materials in the BRE Green Guide to Specification. Accommodation comprises open-plan flexible office space, public areas, meeting rooms and technical facilities. The building utilises a concrete frame for thermal mass, timber frame construction for its internal walls, a timber frame glazing system to the atrium, the primary structure for which – together with the library – is made from glulam posts and beams. The library also has a turfed roof. The external cladding is made from locally-grown, European larch from FSC-accredited managed forests. Untreated vertical boards have been used on the curved library with panels of horizontal boards used on the office facade, the atrium, the top of the stair towers and at high level in the steading, with the shading louvres on the south and west elevations also formed from timber. Internally, larch appears in the atrium at ground floor level and on the parapets of the office floors as cladding to the acoustic panelling. No anonymous office building this, Scottish Natural Heritage's headquarters manages to communicate something of the agency's purpose throughout its form and construction.

> Scottish Natural Heritage headquarters, Great Glen House, Inverness.

Scottish Public Pensions Agency, Galashiels.

At Smithton on the edge of Inverness, the new district offices for Forestry Commission Scotland by HRI Architects are similarly the result of a brief with a demanding requirement for sustainable design. The building was required to demonstrate exemplary use of locally-grown timber, ideally from within 50 miles of its regenerated brown-field site, a laudable ambition to reduce the 'road miles' associated with conventional timber procurement. The parallel purpose here was to facilitate investigation into the wider potential of various species of Scottish-grown timber, a stipulation further defined as the utilisation of locally-grown hardwoods for finishes; locally-grown softwoods for structure and external cladding; and the use throughout of locally-produced board products made from locally-grown timber. Natural methods of modifying timber to enhance its performance were permitted in situations where new cladding opportunities for timbers not normally used for this purpose could be shown. And, of course, unsustainable chemical-based treatments were not permitted at all.

The resulting building is a unique showcase for Scottish-grown timber that rewards closer examination. The design of the main structure, for example, called for some of the Douglas fir members to be 12 metres in length, a size difficult to obtain from locally-grown stock and a problem solved by the Forestry Commission identifying, felling and trimming suitable trees from its own stands on the side of Loch Ness near Fort Augustus. These were then transported to Kirriemuir, home to the only sawmill in Scotland capable of handling such large sections of timber. CAD drawings of the proposed structure allowed a fully dimensioned cutting schedule to be produced, a process that greatly assisted the joiners when it came to preparing and assembling the frame. JJI joists manufactured by James Jones & Sons in nearby Forres make up the secondary structure of the floor, wall and roof, a lightweight and easy to handle solution that is both structurally and thermally efficient. European larch cladding from the Forestry Commission's own woodlands near Fort Augustus is used on the building's gables and on the soffits of the large roof overhangs. This latter feature, together with good detailing designed to ensure sufficient ventilation and good drainage made it possible to use the larch in untreated form for both cladding and sub-frame. Most unusually, locally-grown Scots pine has been used to clad the main entrance elevation. Normally this species is not suited to this purpose, but by using a natural process of impregnating the material with furfuryl alcohol, the timber has been modified to enhance its dimensional stability, durability and insect resistance. The result is a warm colour and an all-important 30 year guarantee to cover its use in this way – a clear fulfilment of one of the main requirements of the brief and a genuine exemplar of new timber construction in Scotland.

Forestry Commission Offices, Smithton, Inverness.

The Laboratory

From the office space to the laboratory, continuous design development has led to increased usage of timber in the modern workplace. The conventional image of laboratories has, since the first quarter of the 20th century, been one of pristine clinical environments housed in steel and glass architecture as logical and rigorous in its form and component parts as the research being carried out inside. This approach to design – representative of an architectural aesthetic founded in precision engineering and continuous technological development – has invariably placed considerations of form and function well above those of context and environment. Nowadays, however, additional factors impact on a building's design: energy efficiency, whole life costing of building components and materials together with the health and safety conditions of the workplace to name just a few. This is especially the case in laboratory projects since they are conceived for highly particular purposes. Many of these buildings are location-specific, i.e. they need to be close to the subject of their research, with sites that demand design solutions responsive to both climate and landscape. And, in a number of recent examples, timber has provided the mediation point between function and external appearance.

At Rowardennan, phase one of the new facilities designed to replace Glasgow University's existing field station for SCENE, the Scottish Centre for Ecology and the Natural Environment by Page\Park Architects, sits within the Loch Lomond and Trossachs National Park and is subject to the very particular planning conditions associated with this area. The land is also designated as a Site of Special Scientific Interest and as a Special Area for Conservation. In such a sensitive location, sustainability naturally ranked high on the list of client requirements, and inspiration for the new BREEAM-assessed project was found in the forms of traditional agricultural barns. The building's basement accommodates a fish holding area and

Scene Field Station,
Rowardennan, Loch Lomond.

35

an artificial stream, its ground floor houses the research laboratories, offices and meeting rooms and the roof space contains a number of study-bedrooms for students taking part in residential courses. Specified for their ability to weather harmoniously with the surrounding landscape, natural stone, slate and timber have been used to enclose the research element of the field station: the east courtyard wall being faced in stone from the Lake District, while the west elevation fronting onto the forest is clad to impressive effect with vertically-fixed western red cedar boards.

Concerns about the effects of weather are never faraway though when it comes to the specification of materials. The marine climate on Scotland's west coast can be particularly unforgiving on the detailing and construction of buildings: if either is poor, horizontally-driven rain can penetrate into the fabric relatively quickly and with inevitable consequences. For this reason, it has sometimes been asserted – inaccurately – that timber is an unsuitable material to use in exposed locations in Scotland. There is, however, no good reason why external cladding should deteriorate or permit ingress of water if its specification and detailing have been carefully thought through and its construction quality properly monitored and maintained. The Scottish Association for Marine Science's laboratory on the coast at Dunstaffnage near Oban is an excellent example of a large building complex with extensive areas of western red cedar cladding performing and weathering well in a very exposed location. Architects SMC Davis Duncan's reasons for selecting this particular species to clad most of the laboratory's facades are entirely sound: western red cedar is relatively impervious to moisture and has good durability; and, when untreated, it weathers to a silver-grey colour which, in this instance, has helped blend the laboratory's four-storey forms into its immediate landscape, and ensure that the building defers in importance to nearby Dunstaffnage Castle.

➢ The Booth Artist's Studio and Residential Space, Scalloway, Shetland.

Laboratory, Scottish Association for Marine Science, Dunstaffnage nr. Oban.

The Studio

At the opposite extreme from the large commercial and industrial workplace is the small studio or office designed for no more than one or two occupants. In previous chapters on detached houses, artists Lotte Glob and Will Levi Marshall constructed workshops for their own use as adjuncts to their homes. At Heriot, in the Scottish Borders, landscape artist Pat Law recognised there were others like her who needed studio space and, rather than construct a building for her sole use, produced a brief for "a gathering place for collaboration and exchange of ideas amongst artists across the creative spectrum". The result, designed by husband Andy Law of Reiach and Hall Architects, is Heriot Toun Studio, a purpose-built eco-friendly live-work space on a south-east facing site in the Moorfoot Hills overlooking the valley of Heriot. The expressed need for a space able to provide light, space and inspiration has been met by a 45 square metre studio, sitting room, bedroom and shower room with large north facing rooflights and a glass sliding door looking onto the hills. The studio's basic form has been kept simple, its 'light footprint' achieved with timber pile foundations topped with a larch superstructure insulated with sheepswool and clad externally with horizontal larch boards. Local planners initially vetoed the project, preferring instead

Heriot Toun Studio,
Heriot, Scottish Borders.

that an annex be built onto the couple's existing house. Eventually, however, permission for the studio was granted because it was to be let out for part of the year to other Borders' artists. Final vindication for this simple timber building arrived in the form of the Chairman's Award at the 2007 Scottish Design Awards.

Not all studio spaces are designed for a specific user or group, however. They can also be generic solutions to an identified need. A striking example is the Booth in Scalloway. Commissioned by the local Waterfront Trust as part of a series of improvement works to the waterfront and New Street conservation area, the Booth is used for accommodation and as a working space for visiting artists participating in Shetland's 'Artist in Residence' programme. The building, a former fishing booth, had become dilapidated and roofless but bold use of colour by Richard Gibson Architects has transformed this small and simple pavilion into a strong visual focus on the water's edge. The joints between its vertical timber cladding boards are protected by a half-round wooden dowel in a modern take on Shetland's historic links to Norway and the type of timber detailing used there in traditional coastal buildings to minimise the ingress of wind driven rain and sea spray.

And finally, workplace solutions produced in response to the needs of individuals can also offer models for similar developments elsewhere. This is particularly so today with modern technology permitting communication to be carried out from any location. This simple fact has prompted more and more people to question their employment lifestyle and to opt instead for some form of home working. In many cases the nature of the daily task requires even a small distance to be created between home and workplace; in other instances a discrete office or studio in the garden facilitates the kind of calm and quiet atmosphere that concentration requires. The studio/workshop designed by architects Crallan & Winstanley to the rear of a Kirkland Street garden in St John's Town of Dalry is an interesting model: a contemporary take on the traditional garden shed or garage, this simple pavilion is sited to the rear of land sloping upwards from an existing cottage. Clad horizontally in western red cedar weatherboarding, the unassuming timber framed volume contains two simple spaces – a large garage and a studio/ workshop with ancillary utility area and WC. A glass-topped verandah to its south face provides sheltered access from the house via large, fully-glazed timber sliding doors. With its underfloor low pressure hot water heating system fed from a gas-fired combi boiler, this is a good example of a high quality home working environment achieved at low cost.

Studio/Workshop, Kirkland Street,
St. John's Town of Dalry, Castle Douglas.

Public Buildings

Public buildings used to be relatively easy to identify: quite simply they were projects for which the client was the public sector, the finance came from national or local taxation and the end user was a public agency. The buildings ranged from council and government offices to galleries and museums, from schools and hospitals to police stations and prisons. In principle, all were in the ownership of the UK public.

Nowadays the definition is less straightforward – for several years, many of the country's 'public' buildings have been developed using financial mechanisms such as Private Finance Initiatives and Public Private Partnerships. Under these systems, schools, hospitals and even prisons have been constructed and operated by the private sector with a myriad of public agencies effectively leasing the buildings and using public funds to pay for their management and maintenance over an agreed contract period. Conversely, 'public' buildings such as museums and galleries that are still financed by traditional means arguably now sit more comfortably within the spectrum of projects defined as 'Culture and Tourism', their design and operation aimed at particular sections of the public marketplace.

Multi-Storey Car Park,
Waterloo Street, Glasgow.

Additionally, there are a number of other types of building that might arguably be categorised as 'public' since they provide premises or services used by the general population, even though they are not in public ownership. A good example of this is a multi-storey car park: owned and operated by a private company, it nevertheless offers a facility that is available to everyone who wishes to use it. Car parks, of course, being highly utilitarian structures, are generally low cost, unattractive in appearance and not well regarded for their contribution to urban form. They are also rarely associated with timber construction, but this may well change if the example in Glasgow's Waterloo Street by MCM Architects is anything to go by. An existing multi storey reinforced concrete structure, the entire facility has been clad externally with long thin 'blades' of Siberian larch layered horizontally on each facade. The effect is dramatic and while it may appear to be a simple solution, a great deal of technical sophistication has been required to achieve the structure's elegant appearance. The timber blades are laminated from front to back to improve their strength and stiffness, with black painted blocking pieces inserted between the blades on the column lines to invisibly maintain the straightness of the overall finish. Fireproofing too, was an important Building Control condition, resulting in the blades being impregnated in a chamber in which flame-retardant chemicals were forced into the timber using pressurising equipment. This particular method of impregnation was selected because it avoided colouring the timber, an important factor as the architects wished the material to weather slowly from its natural warm, reddish tint to a silver-grey hue. The overall change in appearance from the structure's original cladding of mosaic tiles is striking, especially at night when internal lighting shines through the timber louvres and turns the car park into a warm beacon in Glasgow's business district.

Another project that belies traditional definitions of what constitutes a 'public' building is the Recycling Centre at Rothesay on the Isle of Bute. Built and operated by Bute Waste Watchers with construction funding from a variety of public agencies, the new facility designed by Chris Stewart Architects (now Collective Architecture) is itself an object lesson in the utilisation of sustainable methods of design, building and material sourcing. Essentially a processing plant for aluminium and plastic, the majority of the materials used in its construction have been recycled, reclaimed or supplied from sustainable sources. The bricks, for example, are quality seconds that would normally be scrapped but were suitable here for external cladding, their mixed appearance an intriguing contrast to the locally sourced and vertically fixed European larch boards that make up most of the building's elevations. Internally, the cladding of the highly insulated structure is fixed horizontally, with timber posts and roof purlins supporting the metal skin of the roof that was produced from 100% recycled aluminium – the same type used in the cans that the centre collects, crushes and sells on to maintain its economic viability.

Crematorium, Roucan Loch, Dumfries.

Some buildings traditionally regarded as 'public' and operated mainly by the public sector in the form of local authorities are now often built, managed and maintained by private owners. a good example is the crematorium at Roucan Loch near Dumfries. Set within 4 hectares of attractive, undulating landscape, the building has been designed by architects Robert Potter & Partners to take full advantage of its striking location. Hidden from the roadway, the site is bounded to the north by a mature Scots pine wood and to the south by the loch itself. The crematorium is relatively small in size, holding only around 40 people, but this intentional intimacy is complemented by the large picture windows on both sides of the chapel space that provide views out onto the landscape and which, on the lochside, benefit from the natural light that reflects off the surface of the water into the room. The resulting tranquility is enhanced by the careful use of natural materials – the clay pantile roof is supported by a series of curved glulam portal frames with untreated western red cedar used for the external wall cladding and for the framing of the doors and windows. The yellow pine lined ceilings combine with the simple plaster wall finishes provides the interior with a light and airy feel and a warm glow on even the coldest of winter days.

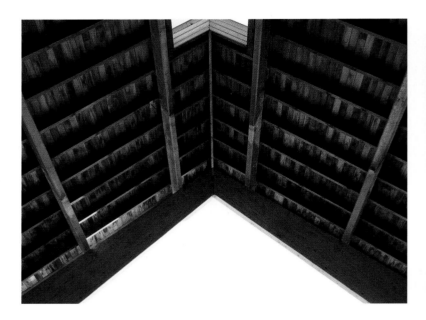

Fire Station, Geisher Road, Callander.

There are surely very few public buildings more suited to the use of timber than a fire station, and Callander, at the heart of the Trossachs – one of Scotland's most attractive areas of forested glens – is possibly the ideal location for such a facility. The two-storey building, designed by Falkirk Council's Development Services to replace the existing, outdated station, does in fact do considerably more than house the two fire appliances and the associated functions required by the Central Scotland Fire Brigade: it also provides vehicle parking and accommodation for the Scottish Ambulance Service together with a publicly accessible and DDA-compliant community space. As well as accommodating the station's service core, the projecting glazed entrance and stairwell asymmetrically separates these functions from the appliance bays, themselves extended by an outbuilding that houses the project's plant equipment. Green thinking lies at the heart of the design – a standard timber frame 'breathing wall' construction contains fibre-based (paper) insulation to ensure high thermal values and low energy usage, with passive stack ventilation and grey water recycling systems adding to the building's sustainable credentials. Externally, the story continues with western red cedar cladding boards vertically fixed to the walls and glulam posts supporting the projecting eaves over the plant room and entrance area.

From fire stations to prisons, both traditional public building types. Her Majesty's Prison at Saughton on the west side of Edinburgh is a typical example of the dour Victorian model that is still found throughout the UK. Outside its front door however, is a new type of 'public' building – the Families Visitor Centre. Financed by the Onward Trust charitable foundation and designed by Gareth Hoskins Architects, the building addresses an important social ill – the poor facilities available to the families and friends during their visits to prison inmates. Saughton can expect up to 1200 visitors a week, but in common with most Scottish prisons its original design made no provision for waiting prior to entering the complex itself. Security requirements meant that large queues of people were forced – often in poor weather conditions – to stand outside without either shelter or amenities. The brief therefore called for a welcoming and comfortable building that could be located outside the prison gates and within which families and friends could prepare for (or recover from) their visits. The distinction between the prison and the visitor centre also had to be obvious to ensure the latter was recognisable as an independent entity. In response to this a truncated cylindrical 'pillbox' draws visitors to the entrance and to the 20 metre long undulating screen wall of cedar and glass that gives a warm and open feeling to the building's cafe space. A series of curved laminated timber beams span the interior volume, each with a subtly different profile to accommodate the inclined angle of the upturned copper roof. In delivering an important prototype, the architects have made inventive use of timber to highlight the difference in the building's functions from those of the facility that overshadows it.

In the same year that they were completing the Families Visitor Centre at HM Prison Edinburgh, Gareth Hoskins Architects' won a competition to design the Bridge Arts Centre in Glasgow's Easterhouse. Six years in the making – during which time the National Theatre of Scotland's headquarters were added to the accommodation schedule – the final project to create an integrated cultural campus comprises a 650 seat auditorium/multi-function space with associated dressing rooms, rehearsal rooms, scenery workshop and recording studio set between John Wheatley College and the refurbished Easterhouse Swimming Pool. There is also a new community library to replace the area's dilapidated public facility. In this instance, timber is not used structurally since the new theatre space's acoustic and thermal requirements demanded the mass provided by masonry cavity walls supported by a steel frame, but externally the whole is wrapped in a skin of Siberian larch cladding panels. The same material is used for both the cladding and louvres of the rectangular box set into the glazed front wall of the library, a device that successfully emphasises the 'bridge' metaphor while at the same time providing a warm, focal element to the entrance elevation. By bringing all of the disparate functions together in one complex, a new type of public facility – a 'bridge' for the local community into performance, creativity and learning – has been created in one of the Glasgow's most underprivileged areas.

➢ The Bridge Arts Centre,
    Easterhouse, Glasgow

Families Visitor Centre,
HM Prison Edinburgh.

Another highly individual public building is the Scottish Parliament in which the debating chamber is arguably the most important space. Designed by by EMBT/RMJM Ltd to have no internal supports, the roof of the chamber is supported on giant glulam trusses that span up to 22 metres from a curved steel tri-girder within the eastern façade to a series of tall concrete masts positioned on the western edge of the space. Secondary elements support the roof above the trusses so that the curved timber-clad ceiling appears to float above the structure. Dramatic towering rooflights, framed in timber, punch push up through the curved roof to allow light to flood the west side of the chamber behind the speaker. The roof trusses are fabricated from laminated European oak connected to stainless tie members via stainless steel nodes. Oak was selected to match the joinery work that is evident throughout the rest of the Parliament complex, and as well as its use in the debating chamber and the extensive use of this material for both structural and non structural elements is particularly apparent in the MSP offices and the garden foyer. The MSP offices feature bespoke storage walls with sliding doors and shelves veneered with oak and sycamore, whilst the central focus of the garden foyer is a series of twelve leaf-shaped rooflights, each featuring bow trusses made of laminated oak 'T' shaped cross members laid on their sides.

The nature of public buildings in Scotland will no doubt continue to evolve in response to the changing needs of society and to new methods of financing their construction and operation. This is important: public buildings are after all the high profile and high budget projects that ideally should facilitate technical and skillbase development and it is essential that they are used to provide the design lead in identifying new possibilities in materials and technologies. Issues of sustainability as well as economic and political determinants are likely to ensure that timber has an ever greater role to play in the form and structure as well as the external and internal appearance of our future public buildings. In itself this is no new thing – timber has after all been used creatively as a quality material in public buildings for centuries – but rapid and continuing progress in computer aided design, timber engineering and the creation of hybrid and composite materials made from wood offers the potential for the next generation of public buildings to be genuine 21st century exemplars of timber design and construction.

Scottish Parliament, Edinburgh.

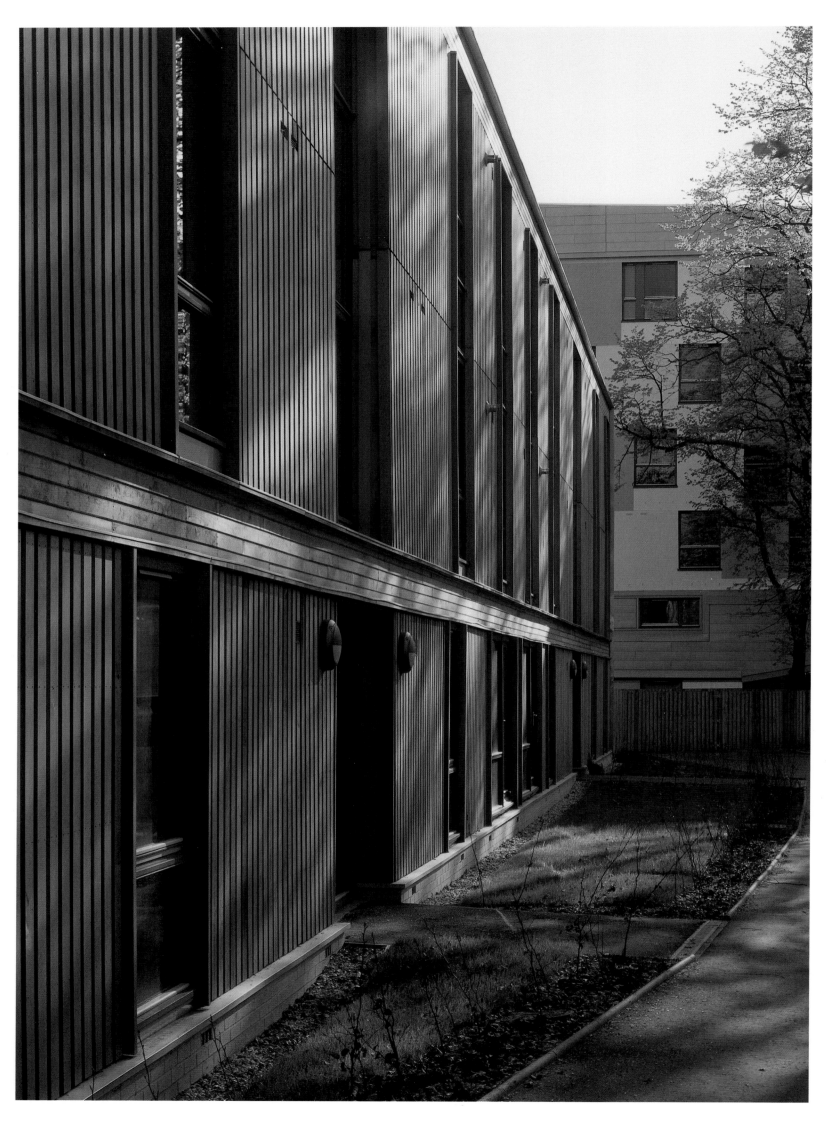

Semi-Detached, Terraced and Multi-Storey Housing

The tenement is the *sine qua non* of Scotland's domestic urban architecture, a building form found in all of the country's larger towns and cities. Not all of these began life as masonry buildings, however, and despite nowadays being concealed beneath a range of other, more fireproof materials, original multi-storey timber framed structures can still be found in the centres of cities such as Dundee and Edinburgh. In recent years, the house building industry has once again brought timber frame to bear in the construction on multi-storey urban housing but, unlike their predecessors, the new examples stand as consummate demonstrations of technical advances in timber engineering rather than as indicators of the size and availability of locally available trees.

Timber frame does in fact form the structure of more than 85% of Scotland's domestic architecture, and this dimension of the country's construction industry can realistically be considered world class in terms of its efficiency of production and speed of erection. To most peoples eyes, however, the bulk of these homes appear to be of denser construction since the outer leaves of their walls are formed from brick or block, reconstructed stone or render. Where visible indication of wood in modern housing exists, it is mostly external, and predominantly in the form of timber cladding. This evidence is increasingly urban, and on buildings taller than two-storeys, indicates the degree to which timber has once again been accepted as an appropriate material for inner-city developments.

Brabloch Park, Paisley.

Just off the Renfrew Road, the main northern arterial route from Glasgow to Paisley, Brabloch Park by Elder & Cannon Architects is a relatively dense residential development set in a landscape containing mature hedging and two major tree belts that are the subject of Preservation Orders. Five blocks of varying scales have replaced the plain Victorian villa that previously occupied the site, with the new buildings positioned relatively close to the existing trees in order to respond to the landscape setting and surrounding context. There are 78 apartments in total, but by dividing them into a series of separate buildings and giving different external appearances to each, the overall impact of the development has been cleverly subdued. An important element in the success of the project has been the use of panels of vertically fixed, board-on-board western red cedar cladding on two of the blocks to tie the project more closely to the adjacent trees. Strips of horizontal boarding has been used along the length of these blocks to break the expanse of vertical boarding on the elevations and to subtly reduce the apparent scale of the buildings. This is intelligent, well-proportioned architecture in which timber has been used to convey a message of high quality finishes.

Still in Paisley, the mixed-use project in Queen Street by Gareth Hoskins Architects for Loretto Housing Association provides a communal day care facility and flats for tenants with and without disabilities. The development seeks to enable families and individuals housed there to participate more fully in their local community. The original perimeter block on the site had continuous facades that addressed the surrounding streets, but periodic demolitions, major road developments, and subsidence from mine workings had led to the townscape losing its coherence. The neighbouring buildings vary in type and scale, ranging from a thatched stone cottage, 2-5 storey stone tenements, a church, and a 16-storey tower block that visually dominates the skyline to the south. In this fragmented context, a building 'in

Housing & Day Centre, Queen Street, Paisley.

keeping with its neighbours' posed an obvious challenge and the design approach taken has aimed to repair the damaged urban fabric by promoting the integration of new and old. A palette of buff facing brick, timber and aluminium cladding is a direct response to the variety of materials in the locale, and a desire for the building to weather gracefully over time. The elevations have ground level plinths beneath a sequence of projecting two and three storey 'pods' that contain groups of flats within an aluminium skin tautly wrapped around the roofs and gables. The hard, urban feel of this solution is mitigated by the introduction of timber-framed panels faced with vertically-fixed, untreated larch cladding.

A similar palette of materials was again used by Gareth Hoskins Architects on a project in Greenock for Cloch Housing Association, Inverclyde Social Services and Communities Scotland. Situated above the town centre, the building is designed for sufferers of Korsakoff's Syndrome, an alcohol induced form of dementia. The layout of the 12 flats and ground floor day care centre loosely follows the former street pattern and has three and four storey buildings grouped around a rear courtyard. The buildings are oriented to maximise views across the Clyde or along Regent Street from the living room of each flat. As with the development at Queen Street in Paisley, the external larch cladding provides warmth and a textural counterpoint to the hardness of the other materials.

Korsakoff Housing, Greenock.

The same reasons might be ascribed to the use of high-level timber cladding on the white rendered Tron Square housing project at the bottom of Fishmarket Close in Edinburgh's Old Town, but here the material is also a reference to the historic architecture of the capital's High Street. Drawing on the practice's earlier housing in the Canongate at the other end of the Royal Mile, Richard Murphy Architects' competition-winning design also looks to the multi-storey timber frame structures of the city's mediaeval period for its inspiration. The Tron Square development follows the original fishbone layout of the closes, vennels and wynds of the Old Town, additionally seeking to emulate the tall, slender form of the buildings that rose from the steeply sloping ground between the Cowgate and the High Street. The result is a contemporary interpretation of the mediaeval paradigm: several floors of flatted accommodation above commercial premises at the lower levels. The use of cedar cladding at the top of the building conveys the impression of successive attic additions, whilst its use in untreated form allows the material to age gracefully within its historical context and obviates the need for high-level maintenance.

Tron Housing,
Fishmarket Close, Edinburgh.

A quite different take on the use of timber cladding on a multi-storey structure is evident on the West Park student housing project at Old Perth Road, Dundee by architects Smith Scott Mullan. West Park is one of four major developments designed to provide the University of Dundee with more than 1000 student study bedrooms, and contains a 19th century villa surrounded by mature landscape. The site is in a conservation area, and in taking its design cues from both the natural setting and the relationship to the historic villa, the building establishes a future development pattern of landscaped spaces that aim to minimise the impact of car parking. The material palette includes brick and copper roofing, but it is the corner timber tower that is the project's most striking feature. Student housing essentially comprises repetitive elements that provide few opportunities for architectural flair and, for this reason, the common rooms and stair towers have been used here to establish the building's relationship with its surroundings and to create a highly visual feature on the approach from the Old Perth Road. The staircases and corner tower are clad with vertically-fixed European oak planks that have been left untreated for both weathering and maintenance reasons.

From Dundee to Scotland's Central Belt, where the idea of the traditional detached villa has been re-thought in the design of a sustainable, energy-conscious residential development in Hamilton by Hypostyle Architects. Another competition-winning project for a housing association – this time Clyde Valley in consortium with Communities Scotland and Hamilton Ahead (South Lanarkshire Council) – the architects worked closely with leading practitioners in the fields of energy and environmental design

to deliver a sustainable development on a particularly tight urban site. To counter the atmospheric pollution and noise emanating from a busy road to the north, a continuous wall of stone is used as an environmental barrier at ground level. Four separate villas containing a total of 26 housing units sit above this base, each with their habitable rooms and entrances facing away from the road. The villas provide a scaled transition from the larger blocks of the town centre to the north and the suburban detached houses located to the south, and are extensively glazed on their south-facing elevations to maximise solar gain. Active and passive technologies have in fact been utilised throughout the project, ranging from communal heating and mechanically assisted passive ventilation systems to solar panels on the roofs, but it is the unconventional form of the buildings and the extensive use of timber cladding to their exteriors that marks out this project as a positive, contemporary design contribution to the townscape of Hamilton.

The idea of raising the principal rooms in a housing project above ground level has been approached in a different way at Fairmilehead on the southern edge of Edinburgh. The site was previously home to the Princess Margaret Rose Hospital's B-listed 1960's orthopaedic clinic designed by Morris & Steedman, architects of some of the finest modern houses in Scotland. Their building took the form of a white harled platform topped with an elegant, stepped black glass superstructure and, understandably, Edinburgh City Council Planning Department insisted that any subsequent development on the site should have ambitions to achieve at least the same level of quality. Malcolm Fraser Architects' design not only pays due homage to the architecture of Morris & Steedman but also manages to take the lessons from their

Princess Gate, Fairmilehead, Edinburgh.

Cottage Flats, Silverhills,
Roseneath, Dunbartonshire.

housing work several stages further to suit 21st century requirements. The development consists of 17 two-storey terraced houses of three or four bedrooms each. These are arranged in five short terraces that step up the slope, culminating in a single three storey block containing six two-bedroom flats at the top end of the site. The buildings ascend to exploit the natural setting, with the principal living spaces in the upper terraces located at first floor level, whilst in the lowest terraces it is the ground floor living spaces that command the uninterrupted view. Black-painted timber superstructures distinguish the two-storey terraces, whilst all three storeys of the rear block are vertically-clad with the same material and coating. The overall result is an elegant, modern housing development in which the external timber cladding is an instrumental component in the success of the architecture.

From the villa to more traditional building forms: inspiration for the design of the 10 cottage flats at Silverhills in Roseneath can be found in the narrow plans and proportions of Scotland's traditional rural houses. Designed by architects Anderson Bell Christie for the Dunbritton Housing Association, this scheme for affordable rural housing has flexible internal layouts intended to facilitate home working. As part of a strategy for low energy usage, the project is oriented to the southwest to make use of passive solar gain during winter months and incorporates solar water-heating tiles in the roofs. Energy efficiency here is also heightened by the use of structural insulated panels (SIPs), an increasingly popular engineered timber product that provides structural framing, insulation, and exterior sheathing in a solid, one-piece component. In this instance the contractor underwent specialist training to erect a Tekhaus SIPS superstructure that, typically, delivers a U-value that is 33% more thermally efficient than demanded under current building standards and has the added benefit in this design of allowing future adaptation for 'rooms in roofs' in the upper floor cottage flats. To give further external emphasis of the project's environmental credentials, panels of untreated, home grown larch cladding are used to complement the plain white rendered walls of these crisply detailed buildings.

Wellington Street, Kirkwall, Orkney.

Even more exposed to the extremes of Scotland's weather than Silverhill's peninsula location is the Wellington Street housing project in Kirkwall on Orkney. Designed by Pentarq Architects for the Orkney Housing Association, the first phase of 35 one and two-storey timber frame homes demonstrates the practice's careful consideration of energy and sustainability issues. Arranged around a central green, the layout and orientation of the four terraces are central to the project's passive solar heating strategy. But it is the development's external timber cladding appearance that is its most obviously striking aspect: on an island with few trees, the long, low buildings are faced with western red cedar boarding that has been coated with Sikkens' 'Filter 7' to give added protection from the elements and to maintain the natural, rich colour of the material.

At the other end of the country, Scotland's sparsely-populated Borders region provides very few opportunities for Berwickshire Housing Association to create entirely new homes, so it is to the credit of the organisation that it has nevertheless managed to developed a reputation for innovation, particularly in the field of renewable energy systems. The two houses at Wellfield in Swinton by Oliver Chapman Architects build on the Association's past work in sustainable technology and detailing. Intended to complete a line of local authority semi-detached houses constructed in the post-war period, this simple house form set within a small garden reflects the layouts of the existing buildings whilst providing a more open facade to the south to catch sunlight and make the most of the views. The energy conservation strategy embraces a whole house ventilation and water heating system and a small glazed sunspace. Well- insulated, breathable timber frame walls are faced in fibre cement tiles and vertically-fixed, board-on-board larch cladding finished with a Sikkens stain to give the timber a rich weathered appearance. The one-and-a-half storey height of the timber cladding strengthens the proportions of what is, after all, a relatively small project and helps to give it the thoroughly modern appearance that, whilst emulating the form of its harled neighbours, distinguishes it from their now sadly tired 1950's style.

Wellfield, Swinton, Berwickshire.

The Extended House

Rising house prices and low interest rates have led to a sea change in the way we think about our living environments. More and more people are choosing to re-mortgage and extend their existing properties rather than move home. Depending on the extent of work required, the price of doing so is not necessarily small but the final result can enhance the living and spatial quality of the existing house and increase its value by an amount far beyond the cost of the actual building work.

Given the range of opportunities the modern extension project presents, it is hardly surprising that highly experienced architects are happy to bring their skills to this aspect of residential property development. In seeking to make real architecture out of even the smallest commission, the simple extension is no longer regarded as second class design territory, but one in which creative people are able to test-bed ideas. It is no accident either that an increasing number of additions to houses have, in recent years, received important architectural awards: put simply, standards in this area are now very high, with some architects even choosing to do only a few high-quality extensions each year. For architects who are also academics, the house extension is now a legitimate area of research into new approaches to contemporary design practice.

Additions to houses can take several forms – side, rear or roof – and can be one or more storeys in height. In some cases they can even be larger than the building to which they are connected. Similarly, the range of materials employed can be wide, often with masonry or steel structures, but timber has a number of significant advantages in both the framing and cladding of small extensions – foundations can be lighter; platform frames and SIPs panels can be fabricated off site, reducing the time required to make the addition wind and watertight; and higher levels of insulation can more easily be achieved than by traditional building methods. And, importantly, there can be concomitant capital and running cost benefits from each of these.

≺ Fernieside, Moredun, Edinburgh.

➢ Gate Lodge,
   near Haddington, East Lothian.

'Dardenne', Kilmacolm

The Brae, Rhonehouse

Larch Sun Room, Granby Road, Edinburgh.

The simplest addition is that in which the structural frame and roof as well as the external cladding are made from wood. This does not imply that this kind of extension is architecturally simple or constructionally crude: it can also indicate a design philosophy that delights in the aesthetic qualities of wood and is founded in a real understanding of the material's physical properties and the most efficient ways to take advantage of its structural capabilities.

A good example is also one small enough in relation to the house to which it is attached to fall within the range of projects classified as "permitted development' and not therefore requiring planning permission. The owners of 'Dardenne', an Arts and Crafts end of terrace property in Kilmacolm, Renfrewshire wanted a family living area more directly related to the large, south-facing garden, a desire met by employing Reid Architecture (now 3DReid) to replace an existing lean-to porch with a single storey extension accommodating the two distinct functions of expanded living space and utility core. The latter area pushes the new garden room out from the rear of the house, where its untreated western red cedar cladding gives the impression of an almost freestanding pavilion centred on the existing rear elevation. The contemporary design of the extension complements both the materials and the strong architectural style of the house it serves.

The simple act of adding an extension can also make better sense of the relationship between an existing house and its garden. The ground behind the Brae at Rhonehouse is at a higher level than the house itself, and architects Crallan & Winstanley have made good use of this opportunity in their response to a client requirement for a new living room, study and dining area. In doing so, additional bedrooms and bathrooms have been created within the existing building. A low zinc roof covers the fully glazed dining room and sweeps beyond to create a covered external eating area at the lower garden level. The living room is set at the upper garden height, with its side wall of western red cedar cladding opening onto a stone flagged patio and its end elevation facing out to an area of timber decking. By clever manipulation of levels, both house and garden have been put to better use and have become much more than a simple sum of parts.

The way in which any new addition is connected to an existing building is critical to its architectural success, and in the case of the optimistically titled 'larch sun room' adjoining an Edwardian villa in Edinburgh's Granby Road, the untreated timber cladding meets the stone wall without any mediating interface. Designed by Reich and Hall Architects, this extension successfully mixes scale, proportion and cladding techniques in its response to the gently sloping site and the architectural form of the existing building. The same architects had already made a virtue of timber in an earlier extension at Cumin Place in Edinburgh, this time facing wood-framed sliding glass doors onto a stepped deck area and bookending the addition with a precisely detailed rainscreen panel of timber. The effect is to give a new sense of balance and enclosure to the existing Victorian villa – a simple solution elegantly delivered.

Cumin Place, Edinburgh

Making a small house significantly larger without damaging the architectural integrity of the original building also requires a degree of subtlety, and in transforming a historic gate lodge near Haddington into a 3 bedroom house, Graphite Studio chose to extend on both sides of the (now) central pavilion. Clad in western red cedar, the two additions give a more balanced symmetrical appearance to the enlarged house whilst emphasising the elegant proportions and detailing of the original stone structure.

Some extensions are larger in conception and more complicated in their relationship to the existing building. At Boswall Road in Edinburgh, architects A+J Burridge raised a rendered gable wall perpendicular to the side of the existing stone-built house. Against this, a stressed skin timber structure designed by engineers SKM Anthony Hunts allows the steep monopitch slate roof to not only enclose a mezzanine office, but also to accentuate the fully-glazed garden room that it appears to float over. The projecting glass entrance providing access to the latter space is balanced visually against the sheer plane of vertical oak cladding by the box frame around the upper storey window.

At Bearsden near Glasgow, architects Studio KAP responded to the steeply sloping site behind an undistinguished suburban villa from the 1950's with a new lower level structure to provide a completely internal link to the garden terrace. This part of the addition acts as a retaining wall to the house itself as well as forming a substantial concrete plinth for the extended kitchen and dining room above. The timber and steel framed structure of this upper (but still ground floor) level is clad externally with cedar shingles which, in the fullness of time, will weather to grey and match the colour of the plinth they sit above. The overall effect is striking and one that has transformed an unremarkable house into a functionally successful and far more interesting building.

An unprepossessing starting point in Edinburgh's Moredun area has, if anything, received even more radical treatment. The late 1950's semi-detached former council house not only has an addition that appears almost as large as itself, but is echoed by a 'contemplation' hut – a kind of home office – that is visually connected to it by the extraordinary landscaping scheme that covers the whole garden. As well as designing the extension, the architect, Graphite Studio's Simon Brims, remodelled the interior of the house and converted the attic: what once had three bedrooms is now a five bed home, complete with an upper floor polycarbonate-lined 'light box' and external deck area. Amazingly, and contrary to its outward appearance, the oak-clad extension is within the 26 square metre limit allowed for permitted development, thus avoiding the need to secure planning permission.

Gate Lodge, near Haddington, East Lothian.

Boswall Road, Edinburgh.

MacFarlane House, Bearsden.

Fernieside, Moredun, Edinburgh.

◁ Linn Park Mansion, Glasgow.

▽ Logie Mill, Craigo.

The opportunity to build a complete additional floor on top of an 18th century building appears less often, but this is precisely what architect Mark Walker of Walker Architecture did to Logie Mill at Craigo in Angus. In response to the North Esk River bursting its banks in 2002, the layout of the traditional two-storey stone house was changed to make the ground floor as flood proof as possible. As a result, a first floor level entrance has been created and is accessed from a new fore stair whilst, to minimise exposure of the opened building to the elements, the timber frame walls and roof were prefabricated and craned into position. The western red cedar cladding and shutters complement the architecture of the original house whilst making clear the distinction between new and old construction. For the owners, the real bonus is the panoramic view over the hills and river from the top floor open-plan living space.

Some historic buildings are of course too large to lend themselves to a return to single family usage and to give them new life, more radical alteration is often necessary. At Linn Park in Glasgow, jm architects along with developers Classical House have managed to faithfully restore a grade B mansion from 1820 whilst dividing the overall volume of the building into two separate apartments. The new extension contains two separate units whose windows are designed to maximize the available natural light and to frame the views of the park from each. And, whilst uncompromisingly modern, it manages to deliver some much-needed compositional balance to the mansion's side elevation. The addition is clad with home-grown European larch that has been coated with a translucent black stain to blend with the surrounding landscape and complement the stone of the restored mansion.

Education Buildings

Education facilities have a unique place in modern society: more so than the church nowadays, the school sits at the heart of the community whilst the economic importance of the higher education sector allows us to talk of "university towns". Buildings in the latter have traditionally been designed for a specific purpose – a veterinary school is, for example, likely to have a very different form of architectural expression to that of an engineering faculty, and these distinctions have become ever more important in the competition to secure students. Put simply, the quality of the campus environment – and the visual appeal of the buildings within it – are critical elements in the modern university's marketing package. This self evident truth has been apparent in North American universities for years, but the UK's quite different fiscal structure has, until recently, largely prevented the endowment of new facilities by alumni and other benefactors. Times change though, and the higher education sector has become much more adept at raising private funds to help develop its estate, so much so that the cost of many of the best developments at UK universities today has largely been underwritten by individual or corporate donations.

Many of these buildings are visible expressions of innovation and technological development and this is as it should be – the academic sector, after all, does not need to build for profit and has both the opportunity and the responsibility to lead in these areas. A good example is Napier University's Business School at Craiglockhart in Edinburgh. The core of the facility is a former hospital building, but this has been substantially extended to provide new teaching rooms, computer laboratories, library facilities and two major lecture theatres. Externally, it is the smaller of these auditoria that provides the new building with visual distinction – a titanium clad, 'egg' shaped enclosure that acts as the connecting element between the old building and the bulk of the new, and which looks out across the capital from its elliptical front window. It is inside, however, that the full extent of the technical innovation

Lindsay Stewart Lecture Theatre, Napier University, Craiglockhart, Edinburgh.

involved in constructing the Lindsay Stewart lecture theatre becomes apparent – the exposed gridshell structure is formed from laminated veneered lumber (LVL), an engineered timber product that has come into greater use in recent years due to the structural flexibility it permits. In this instance, architects BDP working with timber engineer extraordinaire, Gordon Cowley, have created a uniquely elegant structure whose shape interacts with the plywood panels that infill the triangles of the grid to deliver outstanding acoustic resonance.

But it is not just the university sector that is achieving excellence in its new buildings: the country's further education colleges are also playing an important role in pushing the boundaries of architectural quality. ECOSpace at Lauder College in Fife is a demonstration of sustainable building design in action and, as such, a teaching tool in itself. Conceived as a fully accessible, 'green' facility for the construction and energy departments of the college's School of the Built Environment, the building has banks of solar panels integrated into the south faces of the workshop' roof lights and makes extensive use of home grown timber in its post and beam structural frame and larch external cladding. The Douglas fir frame is most evident in the internal corridor that links all the workshops together, the huge sections of timber felled and treated by Carpenter Oak and Woodland. The company installed the structure with assistance from some of the college's 400 construction apprentices. Built on a brownfield site, ECOSpace has breathable walls, a sedum roof and natural light and ventilation. RMJM Architects' design achieved a BREEAM 'Excellent' rating for its environmental performance, but it would be fair to say that it is the visible use of timber that distinguishes it from the mainstream of new college projects in Scotland.

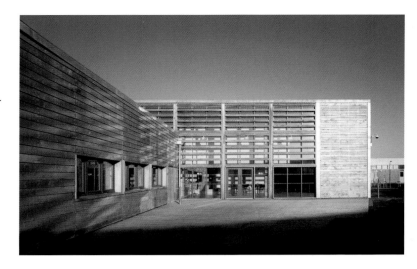

ECOSpace, Lauder College, Dunfermline, Fife.

Auchterarder Community School, Auchterarder, Perthshire.

At the next level of the education hierarchy, a number of schools stand apart from the plethora of new projects developed under the Public Private Partnership funding mechanism. Irrespective of political viewpoints on the efficacy of this particular process, the fact remains that all too few of the buildings constructed under PPP contracts have utilised timber to any degree. One project completed for Perth & Kinross Council before it elected to utilise the PPP process for its new school programme is Auchterarder Community School masterplanned and designed by Anderson Bell Christie Architects. The building replaced an existing school with a new nursery, primary, secondary and community accommodation and had the additional aim of integrating the enlarged complex into the existing fabric of the town in a sensitive and meaningful way. In part this has been achieved by the building's non-traditional form, and in part by the combination of materials employed. With its sleek, curved metal roof acting as a counterpoint to the natural stone and timber end gable of the building's first phase, the external appearance is very deliberately intended to communicate the variety of its internal functions.

The substantial programme of new school building that has taken place in Scotland over the past few years has not been the exclusive preserve of the public sector, however: private schools too have been investing their estate, very often in the extension of existing facilities. St Serf's is one of Edinburgh's oldest independent non-denominational schools and caters for children from 5-18 years of age within its Victorian villa base in the Coates Gardens area, The addition of two classrooms and two science laboratories marked a major development of the school's facilities, a project made more complicated by its location in a conservation area and further protected by villa policy regulations. Reiach and Hall Architects' design responds to the particularities of the context with a long, low building made up of four solid cores that house entrances, storage, and service zones. Between the cores are three spaces but only two functions – the science rooms and the multi-use space. The cores are expressed in white render as a balance to the stone of the existing villa, whilst the science rooms have a band of continuous glazing that sits on a low level rendered wall. But, in this stone-built, inner-city conservation area it is the horizontal timber cladding to the multi-use space that stands out as the most courageous – and successful – of the design decisions.

St Serf's Science Block and Classrooms.

Panels of horizontal timber cladding – this time of Siberian larch – are also a dominant element in the exterior design of Hazelwood School on Glasgow's south side. The building is perhaps one of the most imaginative new education projects in the country, and an important demonstration that, when user needs are separated from inappropriate contractual frameworks, exemplary architectural solutions can be delivered. The design challenge in this instance was far from straightforward – the school caters for around 60 children aged from 4 to 18 who, with dual-sensory impairment, are either deaf and blind, blind and physically handicapped or partially sighted. The site also came with severe constraints, being bounded on the south and east by roads feeding the M8 motorway and by a row of traditional stone villas to the north. The competition-winning solution by architects gm + ad comprises a sinuous, elongated single storey building whose curving plan maneouvres east-west between well-established trees. Simple glulam beams extend between the high level glazed panels to form visible support to the inclined zinc-covered roof and externally indicate the structural rationale of the building. Where full height glazing faces into courtyard areas, external timber louvres diffuse the light and add to the various sensory aids provided by the building's architecture. From the north west, the external perception of the building is one of horizontal panels of timber cladding following the outer curve of the plan and topped with high level glazing of various heights. Other walls are sheathed with a combination of timber cladding and re-used roof slates, the latter a quirky but effective contextual solution. This may be a small school in terms of pupil numbers, but the level of care and sensitivity achieved in its design sets the bar for the standard that should be expected in larger educational facilities.

Hazelwood School, Dumbreck, Glasgow.

On the other side of the country, St Paul's Primary School in Edinburgh's Morningside by the Holmes Partnership successfully demonstrates that even in the world of Public Private Partnership contracts it is possible for timber to satisfy complex specification requirements. The practice has extensive experience of designing PPP schools throughout Scotland, and this track record has been put to good effect here in a demure city suburb that is also on the edge of a conservation area. The demands on the architects to provide a significant route through the site, a public play area and a planning requirement to maximise open green space have certainly been met, but it is the architecture of the school that is the most noticeable feature. On the face of it, the building appears to stand in strong contrast to the surrounding properties, but what is effectively a classical ordering of white rendered base, timber-clad *piano nobile* and timber-clad attic storey gives the school's semi-circular end elevation a dignity and presence found in all too few PPP projects. The vertical timber boards enhance the school's proportions and in time will mellow to a colour akin to that of the stone-faced buildings opposite.

St Paul's Primary School,
Morningside, Edinburgh.

The final tier of education provision in Scotland – the nursery school – finds its modern expression in timber at Flora Stevenson's Primary School in Edinburgh. The nursery sits some way behind a late-19th century stone-built school board building at Comely Bank and contains two classrooms, each for 30 children, as well as general-purpose accommodation. Arcade Architects' design for the nursery responds to a teaching philosophy that aims to allow children maximum freedom of movement between the interior of their two triangular classrooms and the trapezoidal play area beyond. The plan of the building itself forms a larger 45-degree triangle whose longest side provides the nursery with its most clearly articulated elevation and over which an exposed timber roof structure extends to cover an outdoor play terrace. This edge offers the most transparent of the single storey project's facades, and has a clear separation between its cedar-clad, child-proportioned base and the more adult-based dimensions of the continuous glazing above. On its north side, the main entrance to the nursery is enclosed in a cedar-clad box, the horizontal boarding of which continues upwards to shroud the clerestory window and inclined roof plane of the parents/general purpose room. Inside, an exposed steel structure expresses the triangular geometry of the classrooms, a feature further emphasised by inset ceilings of triangular birch ply panels perforated to improve the acoustic quality of these spaces.

Flora Stevenson Nursery, Edinburgh.

Health Buildings

At a time when spending on healthcare in the UK is at an all time high and Public Private Partnerships are the UK government's preferred procurement route for new, larger and ever more complex hospital buildings, it is paradoxical that the architectural quality of this built environment and its effect on patient welfare often appears to be low on the agenda. With the primary emphasis on efficiency through greater centralisation of services, it is perhaps inevitable that some areas of patient care are afforded lower priority than others. These tend to be financially unattractive to private enterprise and the breech is often filled by charitable bodies. Intriguingly, it is this sector that seems most focused on the benefits that innovative architecture can provide in helping to raise the spirits of the individual patient.

Three buildings constructed recently in Scotland show not only what can be achieved by this sector, but also demonstrate the importance of material selection in creating a feel-good factor. With relatively small budgets, each makes exemplary use of wood to develop new architectural responses to patient needs and, punching above their size, suggest alternative, more people-based, approaches to healthcare design.

Robin House, designed by Gareth Hoskins Architects for the Children's Hospice Association Scotland, sits on a steeply sloping plot near Balloch, a small, undistinguished town at the southern end of Loch Lomond. The site offers spectacular views, but located within one of Scotland's new national park areas, the project was designed to sit sensitively in the landscape. The building's distinctive 'ribbon' roof defines the foyer and day spaces by maximising the opportunities for natural light and also provides a variety of profiles externally and internally that have visual appeal for children, a fundamental requirement of the brief.

After exploring several structural solutions, a steel frame and timber substructure was chosen, with economy achieved through repetition and standardisation of components. The four identically profiled ribbons have each been offset three metres in plan to create eyelet windows, the frames of which are manufactured from Siberian larch. The same material was used for the soffits and the rainscreen cladding which, other than the use of a flame-retardant, have been left untreated as it is intended that the walls and soffits will mellow to grey to match the roof materials.

Across the country at Ninewells Hospital in Dundee, Frank Gehry's use of timber in the Maggie's Cancer Care Centre focused primarily on the building's roof construction. Working with local architects James Stephen and Partners and timber engineer and fabricator Gordon Cowley, one of the most inventive wooden structures ever seen in this country has been manufactured from LVL, OSB, spruce plywood and Douglas fir support columns and braces. Standing on a grassy promontory overlooking the Firth of Tay, the concertinaed uneven angular pleats of the building's roof structure not only provide a very visible presence for this small pavilion, but set a precedent in Scotland for cutting edge, complex wooden

◁ Robin House, Balloch.

structures that are able to define a building's purpose. The roof ridge and valley beams are formed from LVL (some being bent in two places) and are exposed in intricate patterns that follow the curves and undulations of Gehry's design.

In this respect, the Maggie's Centres (of which there are currently five in Scotland) form what is arguably a unique building type, being partly educational, partly therapeutic and partly spiritual in purpose. Maggie's Highlands Cancer Care Centre at Raigmore Hospital in Inverness by Page\Park Architects, translates these requirements into built form and connects them into the landscape beyond. In doing so, the architects, with engineers SKM/Anthony Hunt, have exploded what is essentially conventional domestic timber frame construction into complex, non-orthogonal forms.

Inspired by the theme of cell subdivision, the building's design nevertheless fulfils the brief to provide non-residential support and information in a warm, homely, uplifting and stimulating environment to those in the Highland community who are associated with or affected by cancer. The building's form responds to two mounds in the landscape designed by Charles Jencks and, in walls that angle outwards, inverts their vesica shape to create a trilogy of interconnected elements that represent divided living cells.

Initially the engineers conceived the building in concrete, but quickly realised that it would be more practical and possibly cheaper if the complexities – and waste – of wooden formwork were replaced by a low-tech timber frame and panel solution. Working in collaboration with Carpenter Oak & Woodland, the architects and engineers evolved a design comprising laminated plywood chords cut to curve at the top and bottom of each wall with infill spruce softwood and laminated structural studs. In total, some

Maggie's Dundee.

3500 individual timber elements combine to form the stressed skin frame of the building, with the majority of the inclined timber wall panels prefabricated using traditional (but very exact) techniques. A key challenge was how to connect so many pieces of timber since, with each one being a different length, orientation and angle of inclination, the use of standard brackets was not an option. In the end the structural fixing between elements is a custom-designed spliced joint that relies on friction and a hardwood wedge. Internally, a large box beam with a total span of 10.5 metres was used to solve the problem of the four metre long cantilever that projects into the centre of the building. As with Robin House and the Maggie's Centre in Dundee, the overall impression at Maggie's Highlands is one of comfort and warmth and there is no doubt that wood has played a vital part in creating the relaxing, therapeutic atmosphere that is so essential to the success of each.

Maggie's Highland Cancer Caring Centre, Inverness.

The use of timber is not isolated to these highly specialised projects, however, and throughout the country a new generation of community medical and primary care centres have appeared in recent years to change the public image of NHS healthcare provision. Monifieth Medical Centre is one such example – a state of the art, timber framed facility constructed in the grounds of Ashludie Hospital provides accommodation for a medical practice, community staff and a pharmacy together with staff rooms for the Ambulance Service. Campbell and Arnott Architects' design has ensured the preservation of existing mature trees and with the car parking arranged between them to lessen its impact on the site; the relationship to the landscape is further enhanced by the extensive areas of Douglas fir cladding used on the building's exterior. Energy efficiency and sustainability were high priorities in the project's development, the building's narrow plan maximising daylight and its high ceilings facilitating passive stack ventilation. As well as creating a comfortable environment for the building's users, the use of double glazing and high levels of insulation combine with these factors to minimize running costs.

In Penicuik, the same architects have designed updated and enlarged accommodation for the Eastfield Medical Practice and Community Mental Health Team with added flexible accommodation for visiting consultants. As at Monifieth, the design for the Primary Care Centre takes care to avoid existing trees on the site and has resulted in an L-shaped, two storey building. Staff access the facility at the end of each wing, whilst the public enter centrally via a landscaped courtyard. The bright, double-height entrance foyer provides the waiting areas with views to the gardens and trees beyond. Externally the building finishes respond to a requirement for minimum maintenance, with large planes of untreated Douglas fir cladding and timber framed windows contrasting with panels of red and white render and mill finished aluminium roof.

Monifieth Medical Centre.

Eastfield Medical Centre, Penicuik.

Community Centre for Health,
Sandy Road, Partick, Glasgow.

A more urban example of a modern community health facility for an NHS Primary Care Trust can be found in Partick in the west side of Glasgow. Situated on Sandy Road and surrounded by traditional red sandstone tenement properties, the non-residential building designed by Gareth Hoskins Architects is set back from the line of the road to provide punctuation to the streetscape and emphasise its role as a landmark within the community. The contrasting functions of the building and the site's dual aspect have been combined to produce three storeys of clinical accommodation and a nursery at ground floor level. On the street façade, a projecting zinc-clad "box" sits above the glazed ground floor, the horizontal standing seams of the metal echoing the scale of the adjacent stone buildings, whilst the rear façade comprises an untreated cedar-clad box with cedar louvres over the floor to ceiling windows. The building's principal spaces – consulting rooms, large offices, and nursery areas – are predominantly contained within this timber box, itself expressed internally by an iroko wall that rises through the full height of the building. Definitively urban, the Sandy Road Community Centre for Health is a very successful demonstration of timber usage in dense inner-city areas.

In the city's East End and also for Greater Glasgow Primary Care Trust, the Sandyford Initiative promotes sexual health and family planning through a network of clinics or 'hubs'. Sandyford East was built as the first of these and is an extension to Parkhead Health Centre. The rationale for the design by Studio KAP Architects was to deliver a building that would be seen as being welcoming and discreet and disarming rather than overtly clinical, aims successfully achieved by the building's carefully sequenced spaces and a deliberate variation in the lighting and the materials and colours used. By infilling a small corner of an existing double cross plan, the building consolidates the corner of two streets and creates a small courtyard between old and new, thereby offering visitors the option of entering privately through it or via the existing building. The materials used on the building's exterior help to emphasise these options, with the predominantly timber and galvanized steel façade gently screening the more private world that has been created behind the screen of street edge trees. The lapped timber boards also provide a vertical contrast to the dominant horizontality of the single storey building.

The design of buildings for healthcare continues to evolve, with new developments in medical practice and technology requiring architectural responses that eschew traditional solutions. Encouragingly, some of the best new architecture in Scotland is not only in this very specialised field, but is also some of the most original in the use of timber.

Sandyford East, Parkhead, Glasgow.

Leisure, Sport and Retail

Leisure

In recent years, the multi-faceted leisure sector has provided unusual opportunities for distinctive timber buildings. In part this has been down to the sensitive locations that many businesses in the industry operate within and in part a response to increasing customer concern about the environment. Some operators have taken their responsibilities in both of these areas to considerably greater lengths and, as a statement of faith in the quality of the country's native forest products, have chosen to construct new premises from home grown materials. This is not always an easy route to take, for despite the strong connections that exist between timber and sustainability agendas, the reality is that upwards of 80% of the timber used in UK construction is imported. The total embodied energy cost of transporting these raw materials from other corners of the globe (presuming they come from properly certified forest sources) is still outweighed by an equation that takes account of the high quality of the imported timbers, their low production costs and the efficient shipping systems in place to bring them here. For UK-grown timber to compete effectively with this well-established route from forest to building site requires a sea change in the construction industry's perceptions of the availability and quality of the domestic product. It also needs architects and designers to be better informed on the properties and characteristics of the available species if they are to make full creative use of the nation's timber resource.

Waterston House,
Scottish Ornithologists Club,
Aberlady, East Lothian.

◁ David Douglas Pavilion,
Pitlochry, Perthshire.

Happily, the supply chain for UK grown timber has improved immensely in recent years, although some timber species are insufficiently plentiful to ever be able to replace their imported equivalents. There are other barriers to the use of UK-grown timbers, however, not the least being EU procurement rules that prevent their exclusive specification on projects where any form of public funding is involved. Given a list of circumstances that, cumulatively, may appear to mitigate against the use of UK-grown timber, some lateral thinking is required to produce the demonstration projects necessary to convince an often sceptical construction sector.

The new headquarters for the Scottish Ornithologists' Club is just such a project - located on the East Lothian coastline within a short drive of Edinburgh, the building is almost entirely constructed from timbers grown in Scottish forests. Simpson & Brown Architects are perhaps better known as one of the country's foremost conservation practices, but in recent years have completed several modern timber-framed and -clad houses as well as the Scottish Seabird Centre at nearby North Berwick, all of which have made exemplary use of home grown timbers. The Scottish Ornithologists' Club takes this interest - and the case for UK-grown timber - several steps forward. The building's chunky structural frame is formed from Douglas fir and used in its 'green' form to take full advantage of the pegged joints tightening as the timbers dry out. And, by using larger than normal sections, all of the project's secondary framing rafters were produced from C16 Douglas fir, again in 'green' condition. All internal stud walls and ceiling joists were formed from Sitka spruce with counter-battens of the same material, whilst the horizontal and vertical external cladding make use of untreated larch that is intended to weather naturally under the roof's deep, protective eaves. The Scottish Ornithologists Club is an assured demonstration of what can be achieved using home-grown material.

Waterston House,
Scottish Ornithologists Club,
Aberlady, East Lothian.

An equally intelligent use of locally-grown timbers can be found in Perthshire. In 1825 the Scottish plant collector David Douglas made an expedition to Canada and identified the conifer that bears his name. The Douglas fir, together with the Sitka spruce that he also introduced to Europe, together form the basis of today's commercial forest industries in Scotland and his legacy is now commemorated in the David Douglas Pavilion in the Scottish Plant Collectors Garden at Pitlochry. Constructed almost entirely of Douglas fir and roofed with larch shingles, the building is sited at the top of a steep north-facing embankment to overlook the Oriental garden and give glimpses across the River Tummel to the distant hills. The Birnam office of Gaia Architects was asked to create an environmental visitor attraction that would be a focal point in the garden and be built entirely of Scottish timbers in order to demonstrate all that is best about these materials - local availability, versatility in design, sustainability and quality finish. The modestly-scaled building is simple in form but its sophisticated combination of modern concepts and traditional timber joint construction merits greater scrutiny. The roof, for example, is supported on a series of sloping purlins with a 15 m long scarfe-jointed ridge beam that extends beyond the eaves to rest on peeled Douglas fir posts. The 300mm diameter posts stand outside the wall and follow its curve; as a result the eaves are also curved and the resultant roof plane resembles the shape of a delicate semi-folded leaf, whilst the shingles have pointed ends and overlap in a pattern similar to a fir cone. Boiled linseed oil thinned with turpentine was applied throughout to maintain the natural colours of the different timbers.

The work of Neil Sutherland Architects can likewise be seen as a continuing exploration into the use of home grown timber and the practice's recent projects have concentrated on the refinement of Douglas fir post and beam frames with untreated Scottish larch cladding on the walls. In this respect, the non-inhabited and extremely low-cost shelter constructed in a community-owned woodland at Strathnairn near Inverness might best be described as an experimental structure. The new pavilion sits on inexpensive agricultural piled foundations and is a highly articulated exercise in timber structural design. Not only does it have an inventive truss profile within its roofspace, but the bays between the supporting posts are also filled with full height timber 'garage doors' that rise on hydraulic hinges to allow the whole facade to open onto a huge deck area that extends out into the forest. For budget reasons, only the shell of this rudimentary leisure facility has been completed and the building has no mains services. The lack of the latter has perhaps permitted a far more extensive testing of ideas than would normally be possible under Scottish building standards, but it is arguable that this kind of innovation is essential in the ongoing process to discover the full contemporary construction potential of home grown timbers.

Strathnairn Shelter.

The use of UK grown material is not, of course, a prerequisite for the use of timber in the construction of leisure facilities, and many such projects make excellent use of high quality products imported from properly certified forest sources overseas. An example of this type of timber being used to update a period property and create a leisure facility suited to contemporary standards of accommodation can be found in Perthshire. With its secluded position just above the River Errochty and approximately four miles from Blair Atholl, Kindrochet Lodge can be hired for short stays in an area of Scotland renowned for its country sports. The Lodge was originally built in 1820, extended in 1870 and again 1890 before a more recent transformation that - following partial demolition - required a whole new east facing façade to be designed. Using materials synonymous with 19th century Scottish rural architecture, the roof has been recovered and extended to provide a two metre covered verandah. The climate in the area can be severe, with strong north east winds and snow and the slate blue coloured corrugated metal roofing provides shelter and a protected outside space for a wide range of activities as well as a protected rain and storm canopy for the east elevation's horizontally-fixed western red cedar rainscreen. A retaining wall has also been re-clad using European larch to protect and hide necessary but unsightly, stabilising walling beams. All of the internal joinery and windows for the newly-formed elevation have been fabricated from western red cedar.

Kindrochet Lodge, Perthshire.

The phenomenon of cooking as a leisure pursuit has grown exponentially in recent years with cookery schools turning into substantial businesses. Few, however, are found in purpose-built premises as striking as those designed by architect Lisa le Grove for Nick Nairn in the grounds of the Lochend estate on the edge of the Lake of Menteith, just south of Aberfoyle. The original Nick Nairn Cook School was a conversion from a disused piggery into a facility containing a dining room, kitchen, teaching space and offices, but growth in demand for the classes required a doubling in size that has been met by adding a sizeable extension alongside the original. Whilst similar in form, the plan of the new block is set at right angles to a glasshouse at the back of the site rather than parallel to the old block. The result is a link element between the two blocks that is splayed on plan, a design device that channels people into the reception area and shop before a ramp takes them up to the kitchen and the dining room. The use of timber on the new building is very much part of the school's marketing philosophy and intended to communicate the welcoming feel within the school and the tactile nature of the cookery classes themselves. Rather than allow the timber to mellow to silver grey, the shiplapped Siberian larch boards have been lacquered to maintain their golden honey colour and mark out the school as a centre of activity. The result is a crisply detailed modern timber pavilion in which the overall design has seamlessly incorporated the existing building and provided the complex with a scale appropriate to its rural setting.

Nick Nairn Cookery School,
Port of Menteith, Stirlingshire.

Jubilee Park Pavilion, Shetland.

Sport

The sports clubhouse is one of the less well-recorded gems in Scotland's architectural history: simple pavilions whose detached locations, limited budgets and invariably single storey accommodation have made them eminently suited to construction in wood. Many display the form and details associated with Victorian summerhouses and garden structures, others the simple use of materials so redolent of those 1930's buildings whose minimal appearance was synonymous with health and fitness. Examples abound around the country and, whether for athletics, bowling, cricket or golf, no single architectural style has predominated. Many of these structures have reached the end of their natural life and require replacement; others have sprung up in response to demands for entirely new facilities. Inevitably, replacement clubhouses are often that - similar in size and style to their predecessors. Other, more adventurous clubs have exploited the opportunity to create new pavilions that are more responsive to their current and future needs and to the changed physical environment in which they find themselves. Modern sport is also a continuously evolving phenomenon with a number of previously unfashionable or unknown activities for which the quality of training facilities and equipment are as important as an athlete's intrinsic talent.

The reinterpretation of tradition is clear in the Jubilee Park Pavilion designed by Richard Gibson Architects. Located within the Lerwick New Town Outstanding Conservation Area, the building was designed to replace an existing park keeper's hut that had fallen into disrepair and provide accommodation for Lerwick Bowlers' Club, a viewing room for public use, a park games hire outlet and public toilets. In keeping with the conservation objectives, the pavilion maintains a strong horizontal emphasis between the bowling area and the park, its sawn softwood cladding having been treated with an opaque coloured coating selected to match the grass itself. For an apparently simple building, the architecture here has many subtleties, not least in the way that panels of vertically-fixed timber cladding are used to delineate entrances and to highlight externally the differing internal functions. Undemonstrative it may be, but the pavilion's simple proportions and style give it an enduring elegance that places its architecture in an entirely different league from the sheds it replaced.

The opposite extreme in the world of bowling is exemplified by the clubhouse at Balornock in the northeast of Glasgow, an uncompromisingly modern building designed by Studio KAP Architects that provides the sport with a contemporary and youthful image. As in Lerwick, the pavilion replaces a dilapidated structure. Long and low, the clubhouse's main elevation matches the bowling green's west side in length, but is raised above the grassed area on existing banked ground. The gently sloping

< Balornock Bowling Club, Glasgow.

external ramps to the entrance make the link between participant and spectator areas whilst at the same time giving the impression of being part of an almost classical plinth to the building. The sleek horizontality of the pavilion is entirely functional, however, its design having been kept deliberately low to avoid the green being overshadowed in evening light. This is a sophisticated building in which timber is used to dramatic effect within the asymmetrical 'front' elevation. The entrance from the green is deeply recessed under the soffit of the flat roof and is cabinetmaker-like in the construction quality of its vertical timber cladding, a contrast to the strongly horizontal timber framing of the projecting focal window. And, intentionally, the timber provides a warm and tactile counterbalance to the red and white panels of render and to the green itself.

The single storey sports clubhouse is, however, far from being the sole preserve of the bowling fraternity and, necessarily sited in a flat landscape, Stirling Cricket Club's stand-alone pavilion is designed to be seen from all four sides. The low, single-storey rectangular building by jm architects is asymmetrical along both its main axes, a geometry emphasised by the distinctive form of its timber-trussed and metal-clad roof and which itself draws upon the background hills for its silhouette. Deep eaves protect the clerestory windows that are fixed at high level in each of the building's smaller internal spaces, with views from the clubroom enhanced by the full height glazing to the two sides of the corner that faces onto the pitch. Beneath the level of the clerestory, horizontally-fixed boards of untreated European larch form the building's outer walls, a feature designed to blend in time with the grey metal of the roof. The seasonal usage of the pavilion is highlighted by the uncovered timber verandahs that provide external lounge areas for viewing members and players, an element that provides a simple base for the building and which fixes it to the flat green expanse that surrounds it.

➢ Craigholme School Sports Pavilion, Glasgow.

Stirling Cricket Club, Stirling.

In the case of Craigholme School, an independent school for girls on Glasgow's south side, a new sports pavilion had become necessary to replace premises long since deemed inadequate for purpose. The brief for the building called for an indoor hockey pitch with top quality beech wood flooring, changing rooms/storage facilities, a mezzanine gallery and a first floor fitness room. SMC Davis Duncan Architects' design is a *tour-de-force* of timber construction, the key move being the pavilion's striking curved profile, a shape achieved by employing a series of deep section glulam beams to laterally span the indoor pitch and support the aluminium roof covering. Like most sports buildings, this one has a relatively simple plan, but the curved glulam beams have been used here to transcend the pavilion appearing as a rectangular box, and this effect has been enhanced by the skewing of the roof covering to form a trapezoidal plan shape that extends as a canopy over the entrance. At ground floor level, the building's untreated Siberian larch boarding is horizontally fixed in a conventional board-on-board arrangement to indicate enclosure and enhance the building's security provision. This gives way at first floor level to an open joint rainscreen arrangement in which every two wide boards are interspersed with one long narrow batten to create a simple proportioning system.

Craigholme School Sports Pavilion, Glasgow.

Tesco, Wick.

Retail

Major supermarkets are increasingly aware of the need to demonstrate environmental responsibility in their property portfolios and in the sourcing of the products sold to consumers. As a result, a new generation of "eco stores" is emerging, buildings intended by 2010 to consume half the energy per square metre and have carbon footprints at least 50% smaller than those that comparably-sized conventional stores had at the turn of the millennium. Increased use of timber is critical to achieving this ambition, and Tesco in Wick, one of the first such projects to be completed in the UK, demonstrates a radical shift in supermarket design thinking in the use of timber in its structure and cladding. The building itself is a 7,250 square metre single-storey development for which all 1500 tonnes of materials (equivalent to 75 lorry loads) were transported by ship from Grangemouth, effectively reducing the amount of man hours, emissions and road congestion involved in its construction. A glulam frame has been used in place of steel since its manufacture requires only 13% of the total carbon used in production of the latter. Constructionally, the 12 x 18 metre beam and column grid uses standard stock glulam sections, avoiding the need for bespoke manufacturing. Traditional composite wall panels have been replaced with 6.7m high 'Kerto' engineered timber cassettes faced on the inside with standard 12mm birch-faced plywood and 9mm exterior grade spruce plywood sheets on the outer skin, with 200mm of blown cellulose insulation made from recycled paper filling the space between. Externally, the cassettes are clad up to 5.5 metres of their height with 25 x 125 mm horizontal tongue & groove 'Thermowood' boards, and 24mm thick exterior grade birch plywood panels from there to eaves level. With consultants now appointed to monitor and analyse the project's carbon footprint, Tesco in Wick may well be the benchmark for all future 'eco stores'.

But ecology is not only about energy reduction and carbon footprints, it is also about the impact buildings have on their immediate physical environment. Some parts of the landscape are particularly sensitive to the intrusion of buildings, being perhaps of scientific interest, or because their pictorial qualities are of immense value in attracting tourist income to an area. In either example, the relationship of a new building to its site is of paramount importance if it is to avoid becoming an unsympathetic visual intrusion. In these situations, it is not invisibility that is required, but real design skill to ensure the proposed construction is able to complement its location and give new meaning to the position in which it is placed. A good example of this is the restaurant, bar and shopping facilities at Kenmore Holiday Centre in Perthshire, created by Michael Gray Architects. Sitting beside the A827 where the east end of Loch Tay drains into the River Tay and across the bridge from the centre of the village of Kenmore itself, the development had the dual design challenge of needing to be sufficiently visible to passing road traffic in order to attract customers, yet meld into the steeply sloping forest that forms its stunning backdrop. Facing south, the building's simple U-shaped plan creates a sheltered courtyard with deck and lawn onto which the bar and restaurant areas can spill out on sunny days. The scale and appearance of the project have been carefully controlled to sit harmoniously beside an adjacent group of Victorian villas whose architectural style is characteristic of the area. The building's overall horizontality is emphasised by a deep, profiled-metal roof, gun grey in colour to match the exposed elements of the building's steel structure. In time, the crisply detailed, untreated Siberian larch clad will mellow to a similar hue.

The use of timber in the retail sector is not of course confined to rural environments, but fire regulations developed over the past few centuries have, until relatively recently, mitigated against its wider use in more urban situations. This is understandable since, spread of flame is most likely to occur when buildings and/or flammable materials are in close proximity to each other. This is especially so for stockists of timber for whom fire is possibly the very worst thing that can happen, but in the case of Glasgow's East End Sawmills Ltd, the destruction of the public face of the company's main building not only created the need for a new reception area, but also the opportunity to create a shop window for the products stocked in the adjacent warehouse. NORD Architecture has built a reputation as one of Scotland's most inventive design practices, and the new Dalmarnock Road showroom and office it has designed for the sawmill is a ingenious budget solution in which standard timber building components have been rethought to dramatic effect. Conventional roof trusses provide the main frame structure of the new single storey extension as well as one element of its multilayered facade. Externally, vertical timber sections screen the plate glass windows of the main elevation and counterpoint the simple horizontal cladding used to form the raised plinth and roof levels of the extension. Internally, fair-faced OSB sheets are used to line the walls, floor and ceiling and even to form the reception desk itself, an effect the architects describe as "simplifying the form, but also creating an ambiguity between structure and skin that heightens the intensity of the material and the product". A phoenix indeed.

➢ East End Sawmill, Dalmarnock, Glasgow.

Restaurant & Shop, Kenmore Holiday Centre, near Aberfeldy, Perthshire.

Culture and Tourism

Scotland's variable climate has always demanded a different approach to tourism and for many years the staples of golf, whisky, built heritage and landscape have been used to spearhead the drive to attract more visitors. The recognition that greater niche marketing is required to bring visitors on a regular – and repeat – basis spurred the development of a new generation of facilities aimed at informing and entertaining the tourist and the first decade of this century has witnessed a remarkable outpouring of new projects, with several benefiting from the availability of funding from the National Lottery. An attraction's relationship to the modern world needs to be clearly communicated, however, and in some instances demands a unique and memorable visual image that can be immediately associated with existing regional or national symbols. Many of the best examples make extensive use of timber, with their architects bringing a wide range of design solutions to bear on the differing subject matter.

The spectacular landscape of Glencoe attracts large numbers of hill walkers, climbers and skiers throughout the year, a popularity that comes with many environmental challenges. In replacing the existing, inadequate visitor facility and re-naturalising the site, the National Trust for Scotland envisaged an environmentally benign development that could act as a showpiece for its own ecological commitment. The brief to Gaia Architects was therefore explicitly 'green' and the resulting project

◁ Visitor Centre,
   Mount Stuart, Isle of Bute.

➤ Visitor Centre, Glencoe.

embodies a timber frame, breathing wall construction and a biomass heating system fuelled by locally sourced and dried woodchips. Designed in the form of a clachan, the traditional Highland cluster of small buildings, the architecture draws further on local precedent by using the same building materials found throughout the area – the roofs are covered with slate, timber, or corrugated metal whilst the walls are either rendered rainscreens or clad with vertically-fixed larch boarding. Predominantly built with UK grown timbers, the design pays cognisance to the limited range of species available in Scotland. The floors are made from oak and sycamore, the window frames and external doors are fabricated from laminated oak, with Scottish birch, elm and alder used for the internal doors. The ceilings are lined with birch and, because of its high durability, the external cladding and supporting battens are formed from European larch heartwood. The use of untreated timbers renders the building fabric almost entirely biodegradable and the sacrificial use of European larch on the roofs has been accepted here as a key construction principle. With its high levels of insulation and double glazing, the centre is designed to respond to the prevailing climate and its use of locally sourced materials, available skills and intelligent energy strategy make this a very environmentally-conscious and sustainable solution for this important wilderness area.

From landscape to heritage: founded by King William the Lion in 1178, the Abbey is the jewel in the crown of Arbroath's tourist attractions. Following the Reformation, the building's importance steadily declined and it was not until 1815 that steps were taken to preserve the ruins. A 1997 study to examine the feasibility of developing the Abbey as a visitor attraction resulted in a limited design competition, with the winning submission by Simpson & Brown Architects positioning a horizontally-layered visitor facility to the west of the Abbey's high vertical mass. The building comprises three rising, stepping volumes within which each space gains increasing amounts of height and light until at its highest point it finally cantilevers slightly over the rear graveyard wall. Deliberate use is made of natural materials: stone, timber and a green-planted sedum roof. The timber structure comprises a mixture of rough sawn Douglas fir for the built-up posts and fresh-sawn Douglas fir beams for the wall, floor and mono-pitch roof structure. Kiln-dried larch structural decking covers all of the roof areas, whilst the impressive segmental trusses are fabricated from curved sections of 'steady' oak, thus obviating the use of glued and laminated beams. Externally the cladding is formed from good quality, fine sawn Douglas fir heartwood with stainless steel nails used to horizontally secure the untreated tongue and grooved boards to battens. Environmentally-sensitive with low running costs, the building is an excellent example of appropriate, sustainable and distinctive regional architecture.

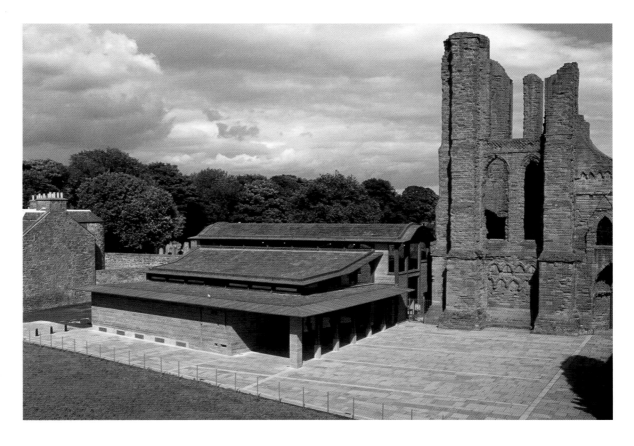

Visitor Centre, Arbroath Abbey, Angus.

The same architects had earlier completed the Scottish Seabird Centre on a rocky promontory beside the old harbour at North Berwick. Exposed to wind, rain and saltwater, the building houses large screens and computers linked to cameras positioned among the colonies of puffins on Fidra and the gannets on the Bass Rock. Visitors to the centre are therefore able to watch the birds in real time all year round without the need for boat trips to the islands. The building is designed to relate to the rugged shoreline and has an unusual form intended to reflect the panoramic views of the Firth of Forth. Given its environmentally sensitive purpose, it is entirely appropriate that the design concept should set out to produce a 'green' building using three natural materials – stone, timber and copper. The north and west elevations are faced with a drystone rainscreen that rises steeply from sea level. The east elevation, by contrast, sits in the shadow of the roof's deep eaves and is a carefully articulated curving wall of vertically-fixed, home-grown European larch heartwood boards. No coatings were applied to the cladding, the preference being for it to weather to silver grey. Simpson & Brown Architects recognised from the outset the potential for the timbers to warp and slightly twist, and detailed the building accordingly.

Another visitor facility designed to weather naturally but which uses a very different timber species - iroko – can be found at Mount Stuart on the Isle of Bute. Here the building is very much a portal to the stunning gardens that surround one of Scotland's 'must sees': Robert Rowand Anderson's magnificent Gothic revival palace designed for the third Marquess of Bute is unquestionably one of the architect's masterpieces. The need to manage increased visitor numbers more efficiently and to provide them with a more informed visitor experience led to the commissioning of Munkenbeck & Marshall Architects to design an entrance building containing ticketing facilities, shop, exhibition space and audio visual displays with an upstairs restaurant and lounge area offering a 300 degree panoramic view over the estate's forest, gardens and pastures. Located on a field stone wall at the boundary between the grazing land and the dense forest of huge trees that predate the house by several hundred years, the building's upper level of frameless glass and aluminium 'wing' roof appears to hover over the angled iroko sections that form the rainscreen walls of the ground floor. The 'wing' itself is constructed as a prefabricated 'egg crate' from very thin, light plywood, with its top and bottom surfaces glued and screwed to these light ribs to produce a stressed skin similar to the type used in the hulls of offshore racing powerboats.

➤ Birnam Institute, Birnam, Perthshire.

≺ Scottish Seabird Centre, North Berwick.

➤ Visitor Centre, Mount Stuart, Isle of Bute.

A more visible relationship to an existing stone structure can be seen in Birnam in Perthshire where MacMon Architects' timber clad extension to the Birnam Institute contrasts well with the stone and slate architecture of the existing building that had provided the community with its hall and lending library for more than 100 years. A fully-glazed double height link now connects it with a foyer and cafe space, multi-purpose hall, arts workshops and a mezzanine gallery as well as a permanent display about Beatrix Potter, a frequent visitor to the area. Externally, however, it is the building's curved, western red cedar clad walls that distinguish it from its older neighbour. The design for radiused ends to the extension introduced a degree of complexity and structural discontinuity to the project that mitigated against breathing wall construction. As a result the building has a steel frame with timber frame infill forming an inner wall leaf and supporting sheathing ply and membranes. The cladding is formed from tongue and grooved boards fixed vertically around the curved end walls. The fixings themselves had to be carefully considered to avoid the groove width 'opening up', with the result that the boards are twice nailed with one secret fixing and one face-fixed. What may very well seem to passers-by to be a simple building form is in fact a complex exercise in timber cladding design.

Technical ingenuity comes no more complex than at the Falkirk Wheel, a revolutionary boat lift connecting the Union Canal with the Forth and Clyde Canal. The focal point of the Millennium Link project, a £74 million investment to join the west and east coasts of Scotland with an inland waterway, the Wheel is architect RMJM's spectacular solution to the physical problem of two canals meeting at different levels. The Wheel is the world's first rotating boatlift and as such has become a major attraction. A cedar-clad, wedge-shaped visitor centre sits alongside and was built at the same time as the main structure itself in anticipation of the huge numbers travelling to the site. The visitor centre is in fact designed as a segment of a sphere, its inner face fully glazed to allow the public to view the Wheel in action, whatever the weather. The outer face of the building curves in two directions and the untreated cedar boards are fixed radially in response to the unusual geometry. The centre's deliberately simple form successfully focuses visitor attention on the main attraction and as a result the technical expertise applied to detailing and fixing the double curvature of the building's cladding generally escapes notice.

Falkirk Wheel Visitor Centre.

At Wester Kittochside farm near East Kilbride, by contrast, the National Museum of Rural Life by Page\ Park Architects appears to avoid design complexity, its form originating in the simple agricultural antecedent of the steading and the idea of barns arranged around a courtyard. The building therefore features a central store and internal courtyard surrounded by the exhibition 'barns'. The Museum has one of the best collection of combine harvesters in Europe, plus a collection of over 100 design concept models of early farm machinery and a whole range of horse-drawn farming implements such as reapers, binders and ploughs dating from the 19870's to the 1950's. With such a wealth of material, the Museum is able to demonstrate not only domestic agricultural development and revolution, but how the past has shaped the way we are now. The visitor follows a spiral route around the world's oldest threshing mill – the only fixed object in the Museum – before descending to an exit to the path that leads up to the old farm steading. Externally, the huge sliding doors to the entrance barn are approached across a simple bridge. The vertical timber cladding to the barn walls is open-jointed, again a deliberate reminder of the natural ventilation achieved in traditional buildings through the use of widely spaced boards.

The National Museum of Rural Life, East Kilbride.

The final example is also the most recently constructed: the Shetland Museum and Archives building sits on the historic Hay's Dock in the centre of Lerwick. Designed by BDP Architects, the museum is home to a collection of more than 3000 artefacts from a working lighthouse to delicate Fair Isle knitting and Shetland lace, plus archaeological specimens from the Picts, Vikings and all those who have inhabited the islands over the centuries. With its cafe/restaurant, gift shop, education room, auditorium and temporary exhibition space, the building is destined to be an important cultural hub for islanders and visitors and for those interested in the preservation and future development of Shetland's wider heritage and culture, there is also an archive search room and boat restoration sheds. Closer to Bergen in Norway than to Scotland's capital, Shetland has a strong Norse influence that is reflected in the culture, dialect and place names of the islands and is uniquely positioned at the crossroads of several sea routes. It is this latter characteristic that gives the building its most distinctive feature: a three storey, sail-shaped Boat Hall containing five traditional boats suspended in mid-air. Externally, the massive inclined trapezoidal planes that enclose the space are clad with panels of horizontal boards, themselves a memory of traditional boat building techniques. Hardly a conventional building form, the Boat Hall nevertheless signals the museum's contemporary credentials and provides it with a defining image that has already become a central feature of the institution's promotional material.

The examples above demonstrate a range of approaches to the design of cultural and tourism facilities that are predicated on the idea of creating sustainable and distinctive regional forms of architecture. In doing so, they also show how an integrated approach to tourism and the environment can have significant ecological, economic and cultural benefits and how designing with timber ticks all of these boxes.

Shetland Museum and Archives, Lerwick.

Featured Buildings and Credits

The Detached House in the North

Lotte Glob House, Loch Eriboll, Durness, Sutherland, 2004
Gokay Deveci
www.rgu.ac.uk/sss/research
Photography: Andrew Lee; Lotte Glob

'Ceol Mara', Loch Broom, Wester Ross, 2005
Bernard Planterose, Northwoods Design
www.northwoodsdesign.co.uk
Photography: Andrew Lee

Guest House, Harrapool, Isle of Skye, 2006
Dualchas Building Design
www.dualchas.com
Photography: Peter Wilson

Shed, Tokavaig, Isle of Skye, 2006
Dualchas Building Design
www.dualchas.com
Photography: Huntley Hedworth

Dickson House, Milovaig, Isle of Skye, 2004
Rural Design
www.ruraldesign.co.uk
Photography: Rural Design

Red House, Ross-shire, 2004
Brennan & Wilson Architects
www.bwarchitects.co.uk
Photography: Brennan & Wilson Architects

Onwin-Lawrence House, Balnafoich, near Inverness, 2007
Neil Sutherland Architects
www.organicbuildings.com
Photography: Neil Sutherland Architects

Inchdryne Lodge, Nethy Bridge, 2006
Bernard Planterose and Locate Architects
www.northwoodsdesign.co.uk www.locatearchitects.co.uk
Photography: Andrew Lee

Wester Tombain, Grantown-on-Spey, 2007
MAKE Architects
www.makearchitects.com
Photography: Torquil Cramer

Burnett House, near Banchory, Royal Deeside, 2005
Gokay Deveci
www.rgu.ac.uk/sss/research
Photography: Douglas Gibb

The Detached House in Central and Southern Scotland

2 Kirk Park, Dalguise, Perthshire, 2005
Arc Architects
www.arc-architects.com
Photography: Tom Morton

Cedar House, Chapelhill, Logiealmond, Perthshire, 2000
Walker Architecture
www.walker-architecture.com
Photography: Simon Jauncey

Langwood Barn, near Peebles 2005
Walker Architecture
www.walker-architecture.com
Photography: Simon Jauncey

Leijser House, Balfron, 2006
Studio KAP
www.studiokap.com
Photography: Keith Hunter

Paterson House, Seton Mains, Longniddry, East Lothian 2005
Paterson Architects
www.patersonarchitects.com
Photography: Keith Hunter

The Long House, Kilcreggan, Rosneath Peninsula, Argyll, 2006
Bl@st Architects
www.blastarc.co.uk
Photography: Ian MacNicol

Laggan House, Blanefield, 2004
jm architects
www.jmarchitects.net
Photography: Andrew Lee

The Holm, Orchardton, Dumfriesshire, 2006
Crallan & Winstanley Architects
www.candwarch.co.uk
Photography: Simon Winstanley

The Workplace

Pentad, South Gyle, Edinburgh, 2003
Page\Park Architects
www.pagepark.co.uk
Photography: Paul Sutton

Torus Building, Scottish Enterprise Technology Park,
East Kilbride 2006
haa design ltd
www.haadesign.co.uk
Photography: McAteer Photograph

Business Incubation Centre, Alba Campus,
Livingston, West Lothian, 2007
3DReid
www.3dreid.com
Photography: Andrew Lee

Scottish Public Pensions Agency, Galashiels, 2003
RMJM
www.rmjm.com
Photography: Matt Laver

Scottish Natural Heritage headquarters,
Great Glen House, Inverness, 2006
Keppie Design
www.keppiedesign.co.uk
Photography: Michael Wolchover

Forestry Commission Offices, Smithton, Inverness, 2007
HRI Architects
www.hri-architects.com
Photography: Peter Wilson

Scene Field Station, Rowardennan, Loch Lomond, 2007
Page\Park Architects
www.pagepark.co.uk
Photography: Andy Forman

Laboratory, Scottish Association for Marine Science,
Dunstaffnage nr. Oban, 2005
SMC Davis Duncan Architects
www.davisduncan.co.uk
Photography: Keith Hunter

Heriot Toun Studio, Heriot, Scottish Borders 2006
Reiach and Hall Architects
www.reiachandhall.co.uk
Photography: Reiach and Hall Architects

The Booth Artist's Studio and Residential Space,
Scalloway, Shetland, 2002
Richard Gibson Architects
www.acanthus.co.uk/gibson
Photography: Richard Gibson

Studio/Workshop, Kirkland Street,
St. John's Town of Dalry, Castle Douglas, 2004
Crallan Winstanley Architects
www.candwarch.co.uk
Photography: Simon Winstanley

Public Buildings

Multi-Storey Car Park, Waterloo Street, Glasgow, 2004
MCM Architects
www.mcmarchitects.co.uk
Photography: MCM Architects

Bute Recycling Centre, Union Street, Rothesay, Isle of Bute, 2004
Chris Stewart Architects, now Collective Architecture
www.collectivearchitecture.com
Photography: Andrew Lee

Crematorium, Roucan Loch, Dumfries, 2005
Robert Potter & Partners
www.rppweb.com
Photography: Iain Graham

Fire Station, Geisher Road, Callander, 2004
Falkirk Council Development Services
www.falkirk.gov.uk/services/development
Photography: Peter Wilson

Families Visitor Centre, HM Prison Edinburgh, 2000
Gareth Hoskins Architects
www.garethhoskinsarchitects.co.uk
Photography: David Churchill

The Bridge Arts Centre, Easterhouse, Glasgow, 2006
Gareth Hoskins Architects
www.garethhoskinsarchitects.co.uk
Photography: Andrew Lee

Scottish Parliament, Edinburgh, 2005
EMBT/RMJM Ltd
www.mirallestagliabue.com www.rmjm.com
Photography: Keith Hunter

Semi-Detached, Terraced and Multi-Storey Housing

Brabloch Park, Paisley, 2005
Elder & Cannon Architects
www. elder-cannon.co.uk
Photography: Keith Hunter

Housing & Day Centre, Queen Street, Paisley, 2005
Gareth Hoskins Architects
www.garethhoskinsarchitects.co.uk
Photography: Andrew Lee

Korsakoff Housing, Greenock, 2005
Gareth Hoskins Architects
www.garethhoskinsarchitects.co.uk
Photography: Andrew Lee

Tron Housing, Fishmarket Close, Edinburgh, 2004
Richard Murphy Architects
www.richardmurphyarchitects.com
Photography: Allan Forbes

Student Housing, West Park, Old Perth Road, Dundee, 2007
Smith Scott Mullan Architects
www.smith-scott-mullan.co.uk
Photography: Colin Wishart

Millar Street, Hamilton, South Lanarkshire 2006
Hypostyle Architects
www.hypostyle.co.uk
Photography: Paul White

Princess Gate, Fairmilehead, Edinburgh, 2005
Malcolm Fraser Architects
www.malcolmfraser.co.uk
Photography: Peter Wilson

Cottage Flats, Silverhills, Roseneath, Dunbartonshire, 2007
Anderson, Bell + Christie Architects
www.andersonbellchristie.com
Photography: Keith Hunter

Wellington Street, Kirkwall, Orkney, 2006
Pentarq
www.pentarq.co.uk
Photography: Orkney Housing Association Ltd

Wellfield, Swinton, Berwickshire, 2005
Oliver Chapman Architects
www.oliverchapmanarchitects.com
Photography: Angus Bremner

The Extended House

'Dardenne', Kilmacolm, 2002
3DReid
www.3DReid.com
Photography: Andrew Lee

The Brae, Rhonehouse , 2006
Crallan & Winstanley Architects
www.candwarch.co.uk
Photography: Simon Winstanley

Cumin Place, Edinburgh, 2004
Reiach & Hall Architects
www.reiachandhall.co.uk
Photography: Reiach & Hall Architects

Larch Sun Room, Granby Road Edinburgh, 2004
Reiach & Hall Architects
www.reiachandhallarchitects.co.uk
Photography: Reiach & Hall Architects

Gate Lodge, near Haddington, East Lothian, 2005
Graphite Studio
www.graphitestudio.co.uk
Photography: Graphite Studio

Boswall Road, Edinburgh, 2006
A + J Burridge Architects
www.ajburridge.com
Photography: Mate Gibb; Zoe Maxwell

MacFarlane House, Bearsden, 2002
Studio KAP Architects
www.studiokap.com
Photography: Keith Hunter

Fernieside, Moredun, Edinburgh 2005
Graphite Studio
www.graphitestudio.co.uk
Photography: Andrew Lee

Logie Mill, Craigo, Angus 2005
Walker Architecture
www.walker-architecture.com
Photography: Simon Jauncey

Linn Park Mansion, Glasgow, 2007
jm.architects
www.jmarchitects.net
Photography: Andrew Lee

Education Buildings

Lindsay Stewart Lecture Theatre,
Napier University, Craiglockhart, Edinburgh, 2004
BDP Architects
www.bdp.co.uk
Photographer: Peter Wilson

ECOSpace, Lauder College, Dunfermline, Fife, 2006
Architects: RMJM
www.rmjm.com
Photographer: Peter Wilson

Auchterarder Community School, Auchterarder, Perthshire, 2004
Anderson Bell Christie
www.andersonbellchristie.com
Photographer: Keith Hunter

St Serf's Science Block and Classrooms 2003
Reiach and Hall Architects
www.reiachandhall.co.uk
Photographer: Gavin Fraser

Hazelwood School, Dumbreck, Glasgow, 2007
gm + ad architects
www.murraydunloparchitects.com
Photographer: Andrew Lee

St Paul's Primary School, Morningside, Edinburgh, 2006
Holmes Partnership
www.holmespartnership.com
Photographer: Peter Wilson

Flora Stevenson Nursery, Edinburgh, 2003
Arcade Architects
www.arcadearchitects.com
Photographer: Paul Zanre

Health Buildings

Robin House, Balloch, 2006
Gareth Hoskins Architects
www.garethhoskinsarchitects.co.uk
Photography: Andrew Lee

Maggie's Dundee, 2003
Frank Gehry with James F Stephen Architects
www.foga.com www.jfsa.co.uk
Photography: Colin Wishart

Maggie's Highland Cancer Caring Centre, Inverness, 2005
Page\Park Architects
www.pagepark.co.uk
Photography: Keith Hunter

Monifieth Medical Centre, 2003
Campbell & Arnott Architects
www.campbellandarnott.co.uk
Photographer: Campbell & Arnott Architects

Eastfield Medical Centre, Penicuik, 2004
Campbell & Arnott Architects
www.campbellandarnott.co.uk
Photographer: Campbell & Arnott Architects

Community Centre for Health,
Sandy Road, Partick, Glasgow, 2005
Gareth Hoskins Architects
www.garethhoskinsarchitects.co.uk
Photography: John Cooper

Sandyford East, Parkhead, Glasgow, 2006
StudioKAP
www.studiokap.com
Photography: Keith Hunter

Leisure, Sport and Retail

Waterston House, Scottish Ornithologists Club,
Aberlady, East Lothian, 2005
Simpson & Brown Architects
www.simpsonandbrown.co.uk
Photography: Torquil Cramer

David Douglas Pavilion, Pitlochry, Perthshire, 2003
Gaia Architects, Birnam
www.gaiagroup.org
Photography: Nic Dawson

Strathnairn Shelter, 2007
Neil Sutherland Architects
www.organicbuildings.co.uk
Photography: Peter Wilson

Kindrochet Lodge, Perthshire, 2005
Jamie Troughton & Hugh Broughton Architects
www.hbarchitects..co.uk
Photography: Jamie Troughton

Nick Nairn Cookery School, Port of Menteith,
Stirlingshire, 2004
Lisa le Grove
Photography: Paul Tyagi

Jubilee Park Pavilion, Shetland, 2003
Richard Gibson Architects
www.acanthus.co.uk/gibson
Photography: Richard Gibson

Balornock Bowling Club, Glasgow, 2006
Studio KAP Architects
www.studiokap
Photography: Keith Hunter

Stirling Cricket Club, Stirling, 2007
jm architects
www.jmarchitects.net
Photographer: Andrew Lee

Craigholme School Sports Pavilion, Glasgow, 2007
SMC Davis Duncan Architects
www.davisduncan.co.uk
Photography: Keith Hunter

Tesco, Wick, 2006
Ian Burke Associates
Photography: Keith Hunter

Restaurant & Shop, Kenmore Holiday Centre,
near Aberfeldy, Perthshire, 2005
Michael Gray Architects
www.michaelgrayarchitects.co.uk
Photography: Michael Murray/Paul Grillo

East End Sawmill, Dalmarnock, Glasgow, 2006
NORD Architecture
www.nordarchitecture.com
Photography: Andrew Lee

Culture and Tourism

Visitor Centre, Glencoe, 2000
Gaia Architects
www.gaiagroup.org
Photography: Peter Wilson

Visitor Centre, Arbroath Abbey, Angus, 2001
Simpson & Brown Architects
www.simpsonandbrown.co.uk
Photography: Keith Hunter

Scottish Seabird Centre, North Berwick, 2001
Simpson & Brown Architects
www.simpsonandbrown.co.uk
Photography: Keith Hunter

Visitor Centre, Mount Stuart, Isle of Bute, 2001
Munkenbeck & Marshall Architects
www.mandm.uk.com
Photography: Keith Hunter/Peter Wilson

Birnam Institute, Birnam, Perthshire 2003
Macmon Architects
www.macmon.co.uk
Photography: Peter Wilson

Falkirk Wheel Visitor Centre, 2003
RMJM
www.rmjm.com
Photography: Matt Laver

The National Museum of Rural Life, East Kilbride, 2001
Page\Park Architects
www.pagepark.co.uk
Photography: Shannon Tofts

Shetland Museum and Archives, Lerwick 2007
BDP
www.bdp.co.uk
Photography: Mark Sinclair

Bibliography and References

The Scottish Government – Architecture Policy Unit

www.scotland.gov.uk/Topics/ArtsCulture/arch

A Policy on Architecture
2001   ISBN 0-755900-59-6

Building our Future – Scotland's School Estate
2003   ISBN 0-755908-55-6

Building our Future – Sustainability
2004   ISBN 0-755943-35-X

Building our Legacy – Statement on Scotland's Architecture Policy
2007   ISBN 978-0-755952-76-2

The Scottish Government – Planning and Building

www.scotland.gov.uk/Topics/Planning

A Policy Statement for Scotland

Designing Places
2001   ISBN 0-755900-37-5

Scottish Planning Policy

SPP 1 – The Planning System
2002   ISBN 0-755922-84-0

SPP 3 – Planning for Housing
2003   ISBN 0-755923-23-5

SPP 15 – Planning for Rural Development
2005   ISBN 0-755925-27-0

SPP 20 – Role of Architecture and Design Scotland
2005   ISBN 0-755939-15-8

Planning Advice Notes

PAN 67 – Housing Quality
2003   ISBN 0-755907-80-9

PAN 68 – Design Statements
2003   ISBN 0-755908-62-7

PAN 72 – Housing in the Countryside
2005   ISBN 0-755942-71-X

PAN 74 – Affordable Housing
2005   ISBN 0-755939-28-X

PAN 76 – New Residential Streets
2005   ISBN 0-755948-79-3

PAN 77 – Designing Safer Places
2006   ISBN 0-755949-82-X

PAN 78 – Inclusive Design
2006   ISBN 0-755950-04-6

Forestry Commission Scotland

www.forestry.gov.uk/scotland

The Scottish Forestry Strategy
2006   ISBN 0-855387-05-X

The Scottish Forestry Strategy Implementation Plan 2007-2008
2007